Coming Home

Nyree Mannion

Published by Change Empire Books

www.changempire.com

All rights reserved

Printed on demand in Australia, United States and United Kingdom

Edited and designed by Change Empire Books

This book is sold subject to the condition that is shall not, by way of trade or otherwise, be lent, resold, hired out, or otherwise circulated without the publisher's prior consent in any form of binding or cover other than that in which it is published and without a similar condition including this condition being imposed on the subsequent purchaser.

The scanning, uploading, and distribution of this book via the internet or via any other means without permission of the publisher is illegal and punishable by law. Please purchase only authorised electronic editions and do not participate in or encourage electronic piracy of copyrightable material. Your support of the authors' rights is appreciated.

While the authors have made every effort to provide accurate internet addresses at the time of publication, neither the publisher nor the authors assume any responsibility for errors or for changes that occur after publication. Furthermore, the publisher does not have any control over and does not assume any responsibility for author or third-party websites or their content.

EBOOK ISBN 978-0-6450217-4-5

PRINT ISBN 978-0-6450217-5-2

Dedication

To my determined, unwavering, sacrificial mum, who in her own heartache loved us, stood by us, fought for us and by her actions instilled in us to never give up.

Contents

The Phone Call	1
Wake Up	3
Forty Days	11
Coming Home	17
I Hate Him	25
The Answer	31
The Scrap Heap	39
One Thousand Brains	45
Turned Around	53
Crossaints	59
No Room	65
Four Hours	71
The Song	79
Photos	87
Red Sea Moment	93
Fire Works	101
Chocolate	109
No to Cheese	117
Going Back	125
The Open Door	133
A Steady Force	139
Am I Gone	145
Bussed In	151
The Garden	159
The Yellow Envelope	167
Seeing Red	175
Home for Life	183
Epilogue	191

Introduction

When tragedy struck our family, we were forced into unknown territory. It was a journey few had walked and for those who had it was a long, lonely, painful path.

Hope had us believing if we did everything possible, things would get better. As we trudged through the darkness, flickers of light would emerge, inspiring us to keep going.

At every turn a mountain appeared, requiring greater strength and resolve to climb. Having a determined, unwavering mother who wouldn't give up, we overcame obstacles and defied odds.

Upon finding faith new doors opened. I started to walk on two roads. One full of adventure, excitement, and great opportunity. The other requiring endurance, patience and faith as we constantly took one step forward and two steps back.

Amazing people, full of compassion, empathy, kindness and care crossed both paths, lifting our hearts and our spirits. Others would strip away any form of hope with their words and actions, pushing us to fight for justice and fundamental rights.

Both roads required sacrifice, courage, determination and love. They were not for the fainthearted.

My two roads formed into one as history repeated itself. Parents who had fought a battle twenty-three years earlier for their loved one living with acquired brain injury, were facing it again. I sacrificed all that I had to take up the baton they had carried for many years.

With the backing of a community organisation, I advocated with other families until we found a solution.

My story will make you laugh, it will make you cry, but it will also inspire you to trust God, take risks and never give up.

Foreword

"Nyree Mannion has been a great blessing and encouragement to my wife Andrea, me and our family over the last twenty years. Nyree loves God and has demonstrated by life and living that she is the real deal. She is devoted and determined in all that she does. You will be inspired by her stories and her genuine love for God. We highly commend Nyree to you as a person of integrity and believe you will be encouraged and uplifted as you read her book."

– Graham Sercombe (Rev), Director/Evangelist - Southern Cross Ministries & Community Pastor – Wynnum Baptist Church

"Young adults are filled with hope and optimism, embarking on a path to achieve their life goals. Thankfully, they do not have time to pause or imagine what obstacles they may encounter. In no small part shaping this memoir is the story of someone who did not "Make it Home" and the far-reaching effects it had on the lives of those who love her."

"In meeting these challenges head on and faced with many ensuing hurdles, never did the writer lose sight of her beliefs or that she was able to achieve great things within the parameters of these challenges. Her unwavering support, determination and ability to get things done is a credit to her resilience and strength of character."

– Dell Mannion, Mum

"It has been my joy and privilege to have journeyed with Nyree the past three years. She has been a great blessing to me as she has to others along the way. Nyree's enthusiasm for life, her fervour for justice, her compassionate heart, her inspiring spirit and her steadfast faith shine forth from every page of this memoir: Love in action. '1 Corinthians 13:13 Now these three remain: faith, hope and love and the greatest of these is love.'"

– Carolyn Bennett, Educator, Pastoral and Spiritual Care Worker

Preface

About to turn 50, I looked back on my life and realised how much I had encountered, endured and achieved. My dreams were shattered at twenty-one, when my sister suffered a traumatic head injury in a motor vehicle accident whilst travelling down to see me.

I was grief stricken, feeling guilty and responsible. My journey became one of hope and despair as our family learnt to tackle every obstacle that came with my sister living in hospital and health facilities for almost thirty years.

Upon finding faith, new dreams emerged and opportunities opened up. I have done things I would never have considered doing, been to places I didn't know existed, and achieved things I didn't think were possible. None of this would be possible without the support, inspiration and backing of others.

I wrote my story to honour those living with Acquired Brain Injury, their families and the incredible people who seemed handpicked to care for them. I want to thank my friends who lived with a deep faith and conviction inspiring my walk with God and who served with me, celebrating successes and staying close through the painful periods. My story would never have been written without my loving, faithful, determined mum who never gave up.

While I've tried to remain true to stories as they happened, I've had to change names of people, organisations and facilities as I don't want anyone to be able to claim royalties or sue for deformation depending on how I portrayed them. For those who have walked and served with me, you might recognise yourself in a turn of phrase or scenario. If it's honouring please feel free to claim it. If it's not I've avoided real names so you can just pretend it's not you.

These are my experiences and told as I remember them. I was not in any of these situations alone, and I acknowledge others may remember experiences, events and emotions differently to how I recall them.

I hope to raise insights into the long-term impact Acquired Brain Injury has on the person, their family members and their community, and shed light on the lengths love will stretch to endure the hardship of caring over the long term.

My story highlights the support, kind, caring staff give to families who are suffering a loss. A loss that stares them in the face each day. It also highlights the additional trauma a lack of empathy and understanding can cause.

Writing this book has taken great courage. Through sharing my story, I hope to inspire my readers that, in spite of tragedy, you can dream again and achieve anything with love, determination and the support of others.

Acknowledgements

Special acknowledgement is made to
Dell Mannion, Carolyn Bennett and
Cathryn Mora, Veronica McDermott
and Kathy Shanks from
Change Empire Books
who made this book possible

CHAPTER 1
The Phone Call

Brrring, brrring!

The phone pierced the silence of the empty office after closing time.

"Don't pick it up!" my boss called as she gathered up the last files from the desk. "We'll never get out of here."

Brrring, brrring!

I glanced over at the phone. *It can wait until Monday.* I locked the door behind me and headed to the train.

A few stops later I was on my way up the hill to my apartment. *I can't wait to share my Sydney life with my sister Sharyn and her friend Michael who's relocating for work.*

Out of the corner of my eye I noticed my flatmate walking briskly towards me. She wasn't carrying anything and looked deep in thought.

At that moment she looked up and saw me. She burst into a jog.

"You need to come quickly!" she cried out. "Your sister's been in a car accident. Your mum's been trying to phone you."

My mind was racing faster than my feet. I could hardly breathe as I entered the front door. I dropped the groceries and headed straight to the phone. Mum was crying uncontrollably.

"Sharyn's being flown to the Prince Henry Hospital," she managed to utter between sobs. "We'll be on the next flight down." She was too upset to say anything more.

"I'm heading there now, Mum."

My body was shaking, my heart pounding, sweat was pouring out of me. I jumped in the shower. With warm water running down my face I started to refill my lungs. Staring at the bathroom wall my focus turned to what I needed to take with me.

My flatmate was calm and methodical. She called the hospital and mapped out the two trains and bus I needed to take.

On the first train, I chose a seat near the window. My gaze fixed on the moving scenery; I was unaware of what was happening around me. My body rocked as the train rattled along the tracks. Glancing at my watch for what seemed like the fiftieth time, I still had an hour to travel. My mind was plaguing me. *What if she doesn't make it?*

Arriving at the hospital grounds, colours were emerging in the sky as the sun was starting to disappear. My body tensed as I tried to find my way to the emergency department. I asked a passer-by for directions. Unable to absorb the information I followed where he had pointed.

My face was flushed. My hands were clasped. I noticed a lady ahead. *I'm going to have to ask again.* Hearing the anguish in my voice she offered to walk with me. She was quick to detect I was close to tears and refrained from asking questions.

I entered through automatic doors and slowly walked towards the reception desk. The nurse's face was gentle, her voice soft as she greeted me.

"Hello," I replied as my voice quivered. "I'm here to enquire about my sister, Sharyn Mannion."

She flipped through the chart on the desk and slowly looked up. "What was her name again?" she asked.

My hands were moving about restlessly. "Sharyn Mannion," I confirmed. "She was to be airlifted from Armidale this afternoon."

The nurse scanned the chart again and started to shake her head. "We don't have any record of her, I'm sorry."

CHAPTER 2
Wake Up

My legs went from under me. My head dropped as tears flooded the floor. *Has she died?*

The nurse quickly moved from behind the desk to help me. As I looked up Mum, Dad, my brother Phillip and Trudy, a close friend of Sharyn's, were walking through the door. I stood up and ran to Dad. I held him tight, seeking comfort in his strong arms.

The air in the little waiting room was thick. No one was able to find words. I glanced across at Mum, wanting to know what had happened. Her face was serious, her eyes sad. "What time is Shaz expected to arrive?" I asked.

Mum's eyes met mine. She started to nod, her lips pursed, her eyes squinting. "She was supposed to be here at 5:00pm," she answered. Tears were welling up in her eyes. "She's undergone surgery in Armidale and is expected to have further surgery when she gets here." Mum placed her head in her hands and started to sob. I knew it wasn't the time to ask anything further.

Sharyn arrived three hours later than expected.

We held our breath as the night dragged on. Our eyes darted towards the door every time we heard movement. My heartbeat was louder than the clock ticking behind me. I picked up a magazine. Not able to concentrate, I placed it back on the coffee table.

Trudy, Phillip and I walked outside to stretch our legs. The air was silent as we watched the door like hawks.

I turned to Phillip. I couldn't wait any longer. "What happened?" I asked.

His eyes were filled with sadness as he looked back at me. "Michael and Sharyn left Brisbane at 4:00am," he replied. "As they were heading into Armidale, they went through a give way sign and collided with a truck."

My heart sank as the cold night air pushed against my face.

"Who was driving?" I asked.

"Michael."

We raced back inside as we noticed a man in scrubs walking towards the waiting room.

Mum and Dad were on their feet.

"We've inserted a drain into her brain to reduce the swelling," the doctor said calmly. "There's no guarantee she'll pull through. The next forty-eight hours will be critical."

The painful silence in the waiting room deepened. Everyone sat staring at the wall. Wrapped in a hospital blanket my eyes were drooping, but I was too scared to close them. *Will she even make it through the night? What if I wake up and she's gone?*

As day broke, a nurse entered the room. "Would you like to see Sharyn?" she asked as she gently glanced at Mum. "We can allow two family members at a time."

I followed Mum and Dad out the door and watched them as they disappeared down the hallway. Wringing my hands, I walked towards the coffee machine. *How am I going to cope seeing her?*

As I turned the dial to release the coffee a familiar voice rang in my ear.

Daniel, Sharyn's boyfriend, had arrived. He looked haggard.

"How is she?" he asked.

"We're not sure," I replied. "Mum and Dad are with her now." I glanced at Phillip. *We're next.*

An extra level of tension filled the little room as we waited patiently for Mum and Dad to return. I didn't know Daniel well and with such a harrowing night with no sleep I just wanted to hold our family together.

Mum and Dad looked like life itself had drained from them as they walked towards us. Their faces were pale and troubled. Mum grimaced the moment she saw Daniel.

"It's not good," she whispered.

No one could have prepared me for what I was about to face.

Sharyn was lying unconscious with tubes attached to multiple parts of her body and machines blinking and bleeping. Phillip and I sat down beside her. I held her hand and started to cry. I felt tortured by the pain inside. I gently rubbed her arm back and forth, hoping she would wake up.

There was no movement.

The only noise was the sound of the ventilator and the regular beeping of monitors.

Beep.

9am.

Beep.

10am.

She's still here with us. She made it. We made it.

The days ahead were gruelling. Doctors were administering drugs repeatedly to keep Sharyn's body still. Her temperature would rise and muscles would contract whenever they reduced the dosage.

***

We were all drained of strength and energy as six of us were staying together in a tiny unit.

"Do you have to do that?" I asked Mum as I covered my ears. "Didn't you do it half an hour ago?"

Mum stood holding the broom. "I've got to do something," she replied. "I want to go back and sit with Shaz but Daniel's refusing to leave the room."

"He can't do that," Dad snapped. "We all need time with her."

"He's been in there for over two hours," Mum continued. "He's making it harder on all of us."

"It's not good the way he moans all the time," Phillip said. "We're all struggling, but it's not helping Shaz."

"Is anyone else in there with him at the moment?" Dad asked as he put down the paper.

I pursed my lips. "No," I replied. "None of us can stand it. He's too depressing. We've been too scared to say anything. There's already enough tension."

Dad grabbed his shoes. "I'll go down and speak to the nurse in charge."

As I laid down, trying to get some rest, the rain beating on the roof pounded on top of my anxious thoughts.

"It's impossible to sleep," I said as I sat back up. "I need to do something to take my mind off things."

"Do you want to play cards?" Trudy asked as she looked up from her book.

I nodded.

The weather reflected our moods; cold and miserable. We hadn't seen the sun since we'd arrived. We had all left our homes quickly, anxious to get to the hospital and hadn't packed warm clothes. Our spirits were low.

Rent and bills were needing to be paid, holiday pay and sick leave needing to be negotiated, and Sharyn's affairs needed to be put in order. We did what we could by phone but were too fearful to leave her bedside in case there was some change.

"We're keeping Sharyn sedated," the doctor said as we sat in the waiting room holding out for some good news. "We're also going to start intravenous feeding," he continued. "A small thin tube will be inserted through her nose and threaded down the throat into her stomach."

Cringing at the sight of the food I gagged. The thought of the green slop sliding into her system made my stomach churn.

Half of Sharyn's beautiful long curly hair was shaved during the regional surgery before she was airlifted to Sydney. Her remaining locks tumbled onto the pillows.

Mum stood at the top of her bed actioning with her hands. "I can place a scarf around her head and move her hair towards the middle," she said with an optimistic tone. "No one will even notice."

I shook my head as I marvelled at how strong Mum was.

After two weeks the sun finally peaked its way out from behind the clouds. It was enjoyable to walk around the hospital grounds and breathe in the fresh air. I felt the tension in my body easing as the warmth of the sun hit my shoulders. I walked to the top of the hill taking in the beauty of the green landscape after the rain.

At last, I had some space. My head was crammed, being confined to four walls in extremely bad circumstances. My mind became quiet and calm as I sat looking vacantly at the sky. If only it had been a bad dream.

As I returned to the hospital, Mum was sitting outside the Intensive Care Unit. Her eyes were misty, her hands clasped. I sat down beside her and waited for her to speak.

"Sharyn has to have another operation," she said as she looked at the floor. "She has an infection. They have to move the drain to the other side of her head." Tears were flowing down her cheeks.

I didn't move or try to offer any words of comfort as I knew they wouldn't be adequate. I sat quietly until she spoke again.

"They're going to insert a Tracheostomy at the same time," she continued, "as her nose is also infected."

"What's a Tracheostomy?" I asked as my eyes narrowed.

"They'll make a hole through the front of her neck and into the windpipe," she explained. "A tube will be placed into the hole to keep it open for breathing. They've advised a tube insertion through the throat long term may cause damage to the vocal cords."

Tears were rolling from my eyes, my throat constricted as I internally screamed. *Enough! This is so unfair!*

***

A couple of days later, the doctor removed the paralysing drug yet again. For the first time in two weeks Sharyn's brain pressure remained stable.

"There's no way of gauging her long-term recovery prospects," the doctor said. "If she maintains good pressure over the next couple of days, we'll attempt to remove the ventilation. This will be done gradually. We'll do four breaths with the ventilator and monitor whether Sharyn can take two breaths by herself."

I sat quietly staring at the monitors trying to think of things to tell Shaz as she lay silently on the bed. We were feeling brighter and more confident than we had over the past few weeks.

As they reduced the ventilation, I couldn't blink. I watched her chest move up and down as she took her own breaths. Hope started to trickle into my thoughts. *Although it's little, she's making progress.*

She gagged.

"Is she choking?" My thoughts raced.

"What's happening?" I ask.

"Is she okay?"

"It's okay, it's a good reflex to have," the nurse reassured.

Everything was strange and unfamiliar. Our fears intensified as we witnessed another family in the Intensive Care Unit undergo great mental anguish, deciding to turn off their son's life support. He had sustained a traumatic head injury in a motorbike accident.

Everyone was quiet as we walked back to the unit. "Should Sharyn survive," Mum said, "we'll do whatever is needed to nurse her back to health." I nodded in agreement, not knowing what it would require.

Our hope was rising as the prospect of her being transferred back to Brisbane was on the horizon. Having Sharyn close to the family home would make things a little easier.

The ventilation had been completely removed and she was breathing on her own. After a few additional days monitoring her progress, the drain and ventilator tubes were removed.

Sharyn looked peaceful and seemed to be asleep most of the time. Deep down we were hoping she would just wake up.

***

"Transferring Sharyn will be traumatic," the doctor said to Dad as we stood in the waiting room. "A medic will travel with you. The air ambulance is booked to transfer her tomorrow."

Mum had returned home as she knew Sharyn had stabilised and she had many matters to address. Phillip, Trudy and Daniel had all returned to work.

Fear overshadowed me as they wheeled Sharyn into the medivac plane. My nose was running as tears gushed from my eyes. I stood watching my sister get further and further away until the plane was no longer visible. There was no question of staying in Sydney.

I felt so alone as I made my way back to pack up my apartment. *Will she ever make it home?*

CHAPTER 3
Forty Days

The sterile, harsh smell caught in my throat as I walked into the Brisbane hospital ward. A sense of pain and sickness engulfed me. Patients' eyes watched my every step as I walked towards Sharyn's bed.

It was positioned close to the nurse's station to enable close monitoring as Sharyn was still unresponsive. The nurses were talking loudly as the aircon whirred above. Trolleys clattered, competing with the sound of buzzers going off.

I longed for privacy as I stood stroking Sharyn's arm. It was impossible to speak without being heard.

"Shaz," I whispered as I sat on her bed. "Tomorrow's your birthday. I've got a great surprise for you. Actually, I've got more than one. You're going to love it."

My mind was excited as I thought about her friends and work colleagues coming to wish her a happy birthday. *Maybe one of their voices, a song, a smell, a story, a joke might jolt her into consciousness.*

***

Balloons bobbed at the end of her bed. Flowers adorned her bedside table. We wore our Sunday best and the smell of perfume and aftershave filled the small space, making me sneeze.

Gil gently placed the small cassette player beside her, quietly amplifying her favourite songs he had recorded. The room lit up as other patients sang Happy Birthday.

I bravely painted a smile on my face, but desperation was taking hold. *Please wake up. Everyone's gone to so much effort. It's beautiful. Please wake up.*

There was no movement, other than the gentle rise and fall of her chest as she breathed. Her beautiful, long, curly locks were gone. A feeding tube protruded from her nose.

"We'll come and see you again soon, Shaz," her friends said as they started to leave. "Happy Birthday!"

Sadness and grief engulfed me as I drove home.

"Why couldn't it have been me?" I cried as I sat crumpled alone on the floor in my bedroom. "I've seen the world. It should have been me."

My heart was pounding, my eyes flooding with tears.

"It's so unfair," I continued to cry out. "Sharyn was such a kind, gentle, caring soul who would go out of her way to help anyone."

She was helping Michael with his job transition and coming to Sydney to cheer me up. If only I hadn't been so down missing London and family. If only I hadn't been so selfish.

My whole body was trembling. I was rocking back and forth. My head in my hands. I felt so helpless.

So tired.

There was no one to comfort me. My parents and my brother were carrying their own grief.

The pain in my throat was so tight I couldn't breathe. I was moaning, crying. The tension in my shoulders was so heavy I couldn't lift my head.

I hadn't just lost my sister; I had lost my best friend.

And it was my fault.

It was all my fault.

I couldn't find the energy to get up, so I lay down on the floor and closed my eyes.

Chapter 3 | Forty Days

***

A week later Mum and I were sitting beside Sharyn's bed waiting for the doctor. Again. We all had questions needing to be answered.

"Will she come out of the coma and if so, how long will it take? Is the increased eye movement a reflex or sign of improvement? Is there something we can do to reduce the perspiration and clenched fists?"

My heart started to race as the doctor entered the room.

"There's been no change in the swelling," he stated in a calm but firm tone. "Sharyn has had a haemorrhage outside the brain. We're not going to operate at this stage as more surgery will be too traumatic."

He stood quietly before continuing. "You need to keep your expectations in the right perspective. Given the length of time since the injury without progress, we don't expect Sharyn to make a significant recovery."

His words were like a bullet straight to the heart.

Mum's head dropped.

My mouth went dry as the aircon sent a shiver down my spine.

The noise in the room stopped like someone had called a minute of silence. We stood unable to move. Mum sat down beside Sharyn and stroked her arm.

I was digging deeper trying to find something positive, anything but my thoughts were silent.

Mum eventually kissed Sharyn on the forehead and said, "Let's go."

There was no sound in the car on the way home. Mum's hands were tightly gripping the steering wheel, her eyes fixed on the road ahead. The light turned green. The car didn't move.

"Are you okay?" I asked.

Mum's head jolted.

"Yes," she replied as her right foot started to move on the pedal.

"Can I make you a cup of tea?" I asked as we entered the front door.

She shook her head. "I'm going downstairs."

She's heading to the garden.

The garden had always been a safe place for Mum. When we were young, mum would get up early morning and spend time late at night, potting and propagating plants and watering the gardens. It was her refuge.

Everything was dismal. We were all facing the reality of having to return to work and the words from the doctor hung over us like a starless night.

***

Another meeting had been arranged by the hospital social worker. He barely made eye contact as we walked into his office. Brochures neatly stacked in sleeves, lined the walls ready to offer guidance where needed.

"I've had a general meeting with the doctor today," he said nervously looking at the desk. "You need to find long term accommodation for Sharyn."

Bang!

My thoughts scattered like a bomb had exploded.

I had never seen Mum so tense. Her hands clasped the side of her chair. Her face was strong as she stared back at him.

"Sharyn's only been injured forty days," she replied defensively. "She's been more alert the last couple of days. They told me she would be transferred to the other hospital for rehabilitation when she regains consciousness."

He shakily moved a couple of brochures across the desk. "I've got a couple of options for you to explore," he said. "There's also information on an organisation who may be able to give you guidance."

My face was going red. *This guy's heartless. He's gutless. How can they just write her off like that? In forty days.*

"That little prick," I murmured as we walked out.

Mum was silent.

***

Mum visited both the suggested facilities a couple of weeks later with a view of placing Sharyn on their waiting list.

Chapter 3 | Forty Days

That evening we all ate together. This was unusual as one or two of us were often at the hospital. I was scooping my chicken covered in apricot nectar and french onion soup when dad spoke.

"How was the appointment?" he asked.

The colour drained from Mum's face. "It's awful," she replied. "It's full of young people in wheelchairs. We're not the only family suffering."

Her tone of voice softened as her face brightened a little. "The staff were very warm, and the environment was refreshing."

"What's the possibility of us getting her in there?" I asked as I heaped more chicken on my spoon.

"There's an eight-year waiting list," Mum responded.

I stopped eating. "Eight years!" I cried.

"The other place was worse," she continued. "The hallways were dark, I couldn't breathe." Her eyes were starting to moisten. "As I walked through the building, the elderly were lying quietly with their mouths open. The staff were sympathetic, but were not in a position to provide the level of care Sharyn needs. It's no place for Sharyn."

She remained in the hospital ward for another eight and a half months as there was nowhere else. Having contracted Golden Staph, she was being moved to the Infectious Disease Ward.

Mum, Dad and I breathed a sigh of relief as we stood in the room with a push up window. It was only small, housing a hospital bed, a chair, and a small set of drawers.

"We'll finally have some space and privacy," I said as my body relaxed. "Access to outside will be so much easier too, its only footsteps away."

I remembered the time we had attempted to give Sharyn time outside whilst she was in the general ward. It was a long, hard, tiresome process.

Staff would transition Sharyn from her bed to the wheelchair before saying, "We'll be back after our morning tea break."

We would wait patiently, for them to return as Sharyn was required to have a staff member to accompany her.

Time outside had to be limited as Sharyn had spent months with no exposure to the sun. We felt relief being removed from the noise of the ward. The warmth of the sun and cool breeze was pleasing to the senses.

We sat quietly on the bench seat next to where Sharyn's chair was positioned. A small black bird with a blue crest landed on the fence. Swinging its tail back and forth, it chirped like it was singing a song.

"It's worth the wait to get her outside," I had whispered to the bird as we rose to head back to the ward to repeat the process of retuning her to bed.

We were greeted by a number of smiles as we sat in the courtyard of the Infectious Disease Ward waiting for Sharyn to be transferred from the general ward. Patients would pass by as they strolled out for some fresh air. Their skin was an insipid colour, their bodies thin and weakened by disease. Some could only drag their feet as they walked down the hallway. Many of them had no hope of recovery.

Over the coming weeks one young man dying of AIDS took a liking to Sharyn. He would walk down the corridor and visit her most days. He was a hairdresser before being ravaged by the pitiful disease and would pick up her brush and slowly comb her hair. In his own suffering he was moved to do the little he could to help.

Sharyn remained at the hospital for two and a half years. There was nowhere to put a person with such high-level needs. She wasn't just a person with high needs, she was my sister. There had to be another way for Sharyn to live, and we were determined to help her find it.

CHAPTER 4
Coming Home

Mum, Dad and I were sitting with Sharyn in the pergola area waiting for the sister in charge. The lattice was covered in dust, the plastic chairs faded. I sat studying the bee buzzing from flower to flower. *What a nice change from the four walls in the hospital room.*

The sister in charge appeared at the automatic doors, a warm smile crossing her face as she walked towards us. I pulled up an extra chair and placed it next to Mum. She glanced at each of us as she extended a greeting. "How's everything going?" she asked, casually sitting down.

Mum took a deep breath. "They've agreed to help us transfer Sharyn home," she answered. "The senior ambulance officer said transfers of this nature weren't part of their jurisdiction, but they'll do it as a once off." Mum's shoulders relaxed. "He was very understanding. His wife is dying of cancer."

The smile left the sister's face as soon as the words left Mum's mouth. "You'll have to be accompanied by a doctor," she replied in a firm tone.

"I've already arranged a doctor friend who agreed to assist," mum said.

"The visit can be no longer than two hours including travelling time," the sister continued.

Mum smiled. "Thank you," she replied. "We're hoping the dog or familiar sounds will have a positive effect."

There was no response as the sister stood up to leave.

I motioned with my eyes and mustered a smile as she walked off. I had been doing a few quick sums in my head. *Two hours. Sharyn's only going to have half an hour at home by the time they load and transfer her.*

It didn't seem to concern Mum. Her cheeks lifted as her eyes sparkled. "I can't wait to get her home," she said. "Let's get her back inside."

***

There was a lot of activity in the house the day before Sharyn came home. The bay window was full of gifts friends and work colleagues had given. The white bear with the bandage on his head sat in the middle. His facial expression was one of having fun by causing trouble. I sprayed some of Sharyn's favourite perfume before placing the red roses on the coffee table.

I hid around the corner as I heard Mum's car pulling into the driveway. *I can't wait to see her response as she walks in the door.* The latch went.

"Oh, it's beautiful!" Mum exclaimed. Despite her enthusiastic greeting her face was pale and drawn.

"Are you okay?" I asked as she sat down on the double sofa. Something she rarely did.

She seemed distracted as she gazed at the beautiful roses.

"I've had a rough day," she responded. "The sister in charge told me I had to learn how to suction Sharyn's Tracheostomy before she could come home. It was awful; my stomach was in knots; I couldn't stop crying. The sound of the phlegm suctioning through the tube made me want to vomit. I gritted my teeth, determined I wasn't going to let anything stop me from bringing her home."

I stood staring at Mum in awe of the depth of her love for Sharyn and her determination to never give up.

"You're amazing," I whispered. "Surely, it's going to have an impact."

That night, the excitement of Sharyn coming home kept me awake.

Tick.

Tick.

Tick.

Tick.

I have to get to sleep. I rolled over and glanced at the clock. It was 2:00am. My thoughts were racing. *Will today be the day she wakes up? Will the dog, a smell, something, cause her to snap out of it?* I rolled back to my favourite side. *Will they get her up the ramp?*

As a last resort I walked to the kitchen and poured a glass of milk to try and settle myself. Taking the last sip, I glanced down the hallway at the roses. *We've done the best we can.*

I finally got to sleep and the alarm went off.

Sharyn was expected to arrive around 10:45am.

My ears pricked every time a vehicle drove down the street as I hung out the washing.

"They're here!" Dad called as I was heading up the back stairs.

Dropping the basket, I ran to the front window.

"We'd better leave them some room," he said as we stood watching the ambulance men walking to the back of the vehicle.

My heart was singing as they wheeled Sharyn towards the front door. Doctor Rick was beside her.

"Welcome home!" we all cried.

We positioned her chair near the bay window, so she could feel the gentle breeze flowing through. We all scrambled to sit close to her.

No one stopped talking.

"Shaz, look at this," I said as I picked up the bear with the bandage. "It's a soft, white bear, Trudy left for you." I rubbed its soft paw on her skin. "Trudy said to say hi." There was no movement.

I lifted the dog up to see her, hoping the smell and touch would arouse her. No response.

"How about some music?" Mum said as she turned on the tape Gil had recorded for her. She slept through the whole thing.

It didn't stop everyone from smiling. We finally had our own space; the noise and the hustle and bustle of the hospital had gone. We could sit and chat, read or listen to some of her favourite music without being disturbed.

Sharyn was fast asleep amidst the noise. *At least she's home.*

Mum looked at the clock. "The ambulance will be back soon," she stated. "We better start getting ready to go back."

"We need to find a way to get her home more regularly," Mum said as she was heading back out the door.

She didn't waste any time.

***

A couple of days later we were standing in the Toyota showroom. The large space was filled with cars strategically placed on the shiny white tiles.

A stylishly dressed man was walking towards us. "Can I help you?" he asked.

I edged behind Mum a little as she described Sharyn's situation and our need for a vehicle.

"I have just the right salesman," he said. "Please take a seat, he'll be with you in a moment."

The chocolates sitting in the centre of the table stared back at us. Mum glanced around the showroom. "I'm sure they won't mind," she said as she reached towards the bowl.

"This is Tom," the salesman said as he placed his hand on his shoulder. "He volunteers for people living with a disability. I'm sure he'll be able to answer your questions."

Tom listened intently as Mum repeated the story.

"There's multiple ways you can modify a van to make it functional for Sharyn," he said. "They can raise the roof and fit the floor. There are a number of companies who install certified restraints and lifters. You can also have the windows tinted for a little more privacy."

Mum reached for another chocolate as he bounced up from the chair to get her a brochure.

"I've never driven a van," Mum said as she flicked through the pages. "The space at the hospital is very narrow. I'm not sure there'll be enough room to park it."

"They're easy to manoeuvre," Tom replied. "They're a front wheel drive." He must have seen she wasn't convinced. "We have a van here," he continued. "We can take it for a drive and trial it, if you have the time."

Mum glanced at me.

I gave her a nod. "Let's do it."

Tom chatted to Mum about how he started volunteering with people living with disabilities as I gazed out the window. My mind must have drifted as it wasn't long before we were heading up the hill to the parking lot.

"It is narrow, isn't it?" Tom said as he reversed back a little. "It's possible, you just need to go wide before turning." He parked it a number of times before giving Mum a turn.

Mum's hands were shaking. Her head was turning constantly to ensure she wasn't going to hit anything. Tom was on guard, but he walked her through it.

"Can you pick me up later?" I asked mum as we stepped out of the van to observe her park. "I'm going to check on Shaz."

"Yes sure," she replied. "I'll come back after we've dropped the van back."

"Make sure she doesn't eat all your chocolates Tom," I said with a chuckle. "Thank you for helping us."

Mum looked like the cat that had swallowed the canary when she returned.

"We've bought the van," she said.

My mouth dropped. "What!" I shouted. "Are you kidding me?" *You've never made a decision that quickly.*

"By the time I got back to the showroom," she continued, "I was convinced it would work. I rang your dad and he agreed, so we bought it. It will take a while for it to be modified, but we're going to be able to bring Sharyn home more regularly."

I jumped around the room like we had won the lottery.

"You're amazing, Mum," I said as I gave her the biggest hug.

***

We waited four months for the modified vehicle, but it was worth it. Everyone swapped seats as we all had a turn driving it around the block. We waited with anticipation as Mum went to collect Shaz.

The manual lifter had two vertical arms that when lowered met in the middle to create a platform. I released the restraints and wheeled Sharyn's chair backwards.

My heart skipped a beat as I started to lower her to the ground. *What if she tips?* I used my right hand and all of my might to steady the chair. "We made it!" I exclaimed as the platform reached the driveway.

Sharyn had her neck brace on to support her head. Her arms were retracted, her fists clenched, her legs stiff, but she was home. "It's so good to have you back in the living room, Shaz," I said as I picked up a chair to elevate her legs for support.

Mum was moving back and forth from the kitchen, glancing to see that everything was okay. Her face seemed brighter; her body more relaxed.

At lunchtime there was a knock at the door. "I'll get it," I whispered trying not to disturb Shaz.

Standing in front of me was a tall, thin, middle-aged lady. Her hair was short and fair and nicely styled. She was wearing a blue uniform.

Before I had a chance to greet her, Mum was at the door.

"Hello, Dianne," Mum said as she extended her hand. "Please come in and meet Sharyn."

My mind was ticking. *Who is she?* I closed the door and followed them into the living room.

"This is Dianne," Mum said, "From Ava's Community Nursing Service. We're so thankful your organisation is willing to support us so Sharyn can come home."

It wasn't long before they were both heading to Sharyn's bedroom. Dianne assisted Mum to hoist Sharyn onto the bed, change her and position her for a rest.

Chapter 4 | Coming Home

"Do you need anything else?" she asked as she stroked Sharyn's hair.

Mum smiled as she shook her head.

"I'll see you tomorrow then," Dianne replied. "Don't hesitate to call us if you need anything."

We all popped our heads in to check Sharyn regularly as she lay sleeping. The bedroom was just off the living room, darkened by block out curtains. We tiptoed keeping our ears open for any coughing or movement.

"It's going to take a bit of practice," I said to Dad with a bit of a chuckle as Mum was showing us how to change Sharyn and hoist her back to the wheelchair. "I'm sure we're going to get plenty of it."

Sharyn hadn't been back in her wheelchair long when I noticed a strong and very unpleasant smell in the living room. I scanned the room and noticed a large cream puddle on the floor underneath her foot plates.

As I moved closer, the smell got stronger. I gagged. I looked at the mixture in a plastic bag hanging from the pole behind Sharyn's chair. I followed the tube and noticed the attachment that drip fed the mixture directly to her stomach had popped out.

The oily mixture was all over her leg, through the chair and was now dripping onto the floor. The revolting smell curdled in my stomach. I turned the tube off and ran for help.

"Sharyn's had an accident!" I shouted. "Her peg feed is everywhere."

Mum moved steadily towards the living room. "Oh no!" she exclaimed as she put her hand to her face. She went back to the kitchen to get her gloves. "Can you get the hoist please?" she asked, "and some towels."

When I returned, Mum was mopping up the mixture. "Please get me a clean outfit for Sharyn." she continued. "There's one in her top drawer." Nothing ever seemed to unnerve Mum. She fixed things in a calm and orderly manner.

We placed a number of towels on the bed before hoisting her to mop up any remaining mixture on Sharyn's pants. Our only solution was to remove the cover of her seating cushion and replace it with a towel.

It didn't phase Mum. She loved having Sharyn home and would do whatever it took. As I drove her back to the hospital that evening I wondered if it would ever be possible to bring her home, permanently.

CHAPTER 5
I Hate Him

I heard a familiar voice as I entered the front door. I jumped in excitement as I headed to the patio.

"What are you doing here?" I asked. "It's so good to see you."

My cousin Fay gave me a big hug. "I'm down for the weekend," she replied. "I rang your Mum to see if I could pop in and here I am."

We sat listening to her travelling adventures with her husband. I always loved hearing about new places, people and their different cultures.

"Mum's been telling me what has happened over the last year," Fay said as the conversation turned. "We've been praying for Sharyn; I asked the whole church to pray for her the minute we heard about the accident."

I looked at Sharyn sitting in her wheelchair beside us. Having no muscle control, her head was slumped to the side and her neck towels were wet from saliva. *It obviously hasn't made a difference.*

"That's nice," I replied, my eyes darting around the backyard trying to find something to look at.

"Can I pray for Sharyn now?" she asked, looking at Mum.

"If you like," Mum replied.

Feeling uncomfortable I wasn't about to stay. "I'm just going to the toilet," I said quickly as I hopped up from my chair. "I'll be back."

Hiding in the next room, I tilted my head around the corner. Fay had her back to me. She dropped her head as she placed her hand on Sharyn's arm.

I didn't know she went to church. She's never spoken about it. Nobody has.

She eventually sat up and looked around.

"Would you like a cup of tea?" I asked as I headed back towards the table.

In the afternoon prayer came up again. Mum and I were returning Sharyn to the hospital when we noticed George, one of the wards men, wheeling a patient up the hill.

"That's got to be hard," I said to Mum as I saw the muscles tensing in his arm.

"He'd be used to it," she replied. "They do it every day."

"I'll come out and give you a hand as soon as I get my friend inside," he greeted as we stepped out of the van. George returned just as we had lowered Shaz to the ground. His cheeks were rosy. His eyes were kind. He turned to Sharyn and put his hand on her shoulder.

"How has your day been?" he asked looking at Mum.

"We've had a nice day, thanks," Mum replied. "My niece has been down to visit."

He paused for a moment as he stood wringing his hands.

"Dell, would you like my sister to come and pray for Sharyn?" he asked sheepishly. "I'm not a Christian, but Jan is. She believes in God and miracles."

My mouth dropped as my eyes darted in another direction. *Twice in one day.*

"We would love to meet her," Mum responded. "We need all the help we can get."

What? Is she serious?

She pulled a piece of paper from her handbag and wrote down her phone number. "Can you get her to call me so we can arrange a time?"

I stood perplexed. *No one's ever talked about God in our family; there's no Bible in the house and I've never seen anybody pray.*

My mind drifted back to the day Trudy and Dean got married six months earlier.

The magnificent old brick church had stood taller than the trees in the backdrop. The stained-glass windows enhanced the beauty of the setting. Dean wore his usual cheeky grin, his eyes beaming as he waited with his groomsmen for Trudy to arrive.

As I sat in the quietness of the moment, anger rose within me.

If there is a God, I hate him.

I had gritted my teeth, while trying to maintain a smile.

How could God let such a terrible thing happen to my sister? My outward appearance had remained calm but my mind was troubled. *Why didn't He protect her?*

Mum nudged me. "Are you coming?" she asked.

Turning towards her I noticed George was heading back down the hill.

"Are you seriously going to let someone you don't know pray for Sharyn?" I asked as we headed into the ward.

"Yes," she responded. "I am. Prayer helped me as a young girl, and it might help us now."

"How does prayer help?" I asked Mum as we drove home. "Is it some kind of sick joke?" Tears were welling up in my eyes. "It hasn't helped Sharyn."

"My father died when I was fifteen," Mum replied. "My mum went to a nursing home not long after his death. I was on my own. Aunty Mae let me live with her until I met and married your father."

"Fifteen. I'd forgotten that. That's so young."

"I used to take myself off to confirmation classes," she continued. "My friends were all going and I wanted to be like them. I always remember the calm peace I felt when I was at the church."

Withdrawing from the conversation I stared out the window, contemplating how hard it must have been for Mum to lose her parents at such a young age. As we passed house after house pictures of a little wooden A-frame church flashed through my mind.

The building had three little stairs leading into it. Wooden pews were positioned at intervals along both sides of the building with an aisle in the middle leading up to the pulpit. The windows pushed out, making room for a small breeze on a hot day.

Swinging my legs back and forward I would fiddle with anything I could find to pass the time. My only thought had been, *when can I go out and play?* I didn't remember feeling a calm peace.

"Prayer can't do any harm," Mum said as she pulled into the driveway.

I wasn't convinced.

***

Mum and Dad met Jan and her friend Lena a week later to pray for Sharyn. The following Sunday they all went to their church service.

The house was quiet until an unfamiliar car pulled into the driveway.

Peering out the window I noticed a tall man helping Dad out of the car. *Something's happened. He doesn't look well.*

I ran to open the front door. "Is everything okay?" I asked as I looked at the gentleman steadying him.

"Your Dad passed out at church this morning," he replied. "He might need a cup of tea and a rest this afternoon." He gave me a gentle smile. "He'll be okay."

Pursing my lips, I tried to do everything I could not to laugh. *I can't believe he went to church and passed out. That's hilarious.*

Mum rolled her eyes behind him. "Thank you so much for your help," she said. "He's a bit of a worry."

The man's dimples showed as his smile broadened. "More than happy to help," he replied. "I look forward to seeing you again."

I farewelled him with a wave. *Doubt it.*

After placing a cup of tea on dad's bedside table, I headed downstairs to get a bucket. I giggled as images flashed through my mind of Dad falling

Chapter 5 | I Hate Him

down in the midst of a group of people he didn't know. He was half asleep when I returned.

"I brought you a bucket, just in case," I said. "Do you need anything else?"

He shook his head.

Mum was in the kitchen preparing lunch. "You've got to come to church," she said. "It's full of life. Everyone's happy, they sing, and they've all got their hands raised."

My mind stammered as I stood staring back at her. *What's happened to you? You're always so conservative.*

"It's okay for you," I replied in a terse tone, "but leave me out of it."

Over the following weeks, Mum seemed different. She was doing the same things for Sharyn and the family every day but there was a deep calm about her. She was happy, she had a spring in her step and a song on her lips.

Sharyn was also more alert and attentive. Her eyes would follow us as we moved around the house. Her neck muscles grew stronger, enabling her to hold her head up for longer periods without the brace. Despite Dad passing out on the first day, Mum and Dad went back to the church each week.

Deep questions had troubled me for a number of years following a school friend being killed in a horse-riding accident and had multiplied since Sharyn was injured.

Mum hadn't asked me again about going to church, but intrigue was getting the better of me. *Maybe there's something in this. I need to check it out sometime. No one will know I'm there.*

CHAPTER 6
The Answer

Jan was carrying a small box as she and Lena entered the house. *Maybe it's a box of chocolates. Mum will be pleased.*

The smell of fish and roast vegetables were seeping through the house as we sat chatting in the lounge room.

"Jan," Mum said, "can you tell Nyree the story about the young man in the boating accident?"

I gave her a nod as she glanced at me.

My eyes were moving back and forth as my mind ticked. Jan's story of the young man in the boating accident was intense. My throat was already in my mouth. Sharyn sat beside me; her head slumped as she nodded off.

"He suffered a spinal cord injury," Jan continued. "He was unable to walk and was very dependent on others."

Sadness washed over me as her words exemplified our situation.

"His mates would often turn up at his house and take him to church," she said. "One morning there was a visiting preacher. After his sermon, he invited anyone who would like prayer to head to the front. The man looked at his friends giving them the nod that he would like to go forward."

I was holding my breath wondering what was about to happen.

"The people sat in silence as the preacher prayed for him and shouted, 'Stand up!'" she continued. "The man didn't have time to think. He was up on his feet."

A shiver went down my spine.

"The place erupted as he took his first steps. He then started to run back and forth across the stage."

Is this possible, or is it just a good story? I was unable to blink. My mind was racing.

Jan reached for a book in her bag.

"The Bible is full of stories of people who were healed," she said. "It's also full of stories of hope, deliverance and redemption."

My mind twitched. *What's redemption?*

She recited the story about the first couple ever created—Adam and Eve. "They were created by God in the beginning," Jan said. "God gave them the freedom to eat from any tree in the garden, but commanded them not to eat from the tree of knowledge of good and evil, or they would surely die."

"Being tempted by the serpent, Adam and Eve disobeyed God and ate from the tree," she continued. "Their disobedience caused sin to enter the earth separating them from God. We're all separated from God because of the wrong things we have done." She paused.

I waited. I moved forward. *Why haven't I heard this before?*

"God had a plan," she continued as she flicked through the pages of the Bible. "Romans 6:23 says, The Wages of sin is death, but the gift of God is eternal life in Christ Jesus our Lord. Christ Jesus was born of the Virgin Mary; He was fully God and fully man."

I felt confused. *How can someone be fully God and fully man?*

"He was without sin," she continued. "He taught people the ways of God, performed miracles, opened blind eyes and cast out demons. He died on the cross to take the punishment for our sin. Three days later he rose again."

Looking around the room I noticed no one was moving, but my heart was.

Chapter 6 | The Answer

Ding! The stove timer trilled in the other room.

"Lunch is ready," Mum said as she rose to her feet.

My mind was in overdrive as I set the table.

"Do you mind if we give thanks?" Jan asked.

"That will be lovely," Mum replied.

Jan and Lena closed their eyes and dropped their heads. I looked at Mum and Dad who seemed to be following suit. I half dropped my head but lifted my eyes. I didn't want to miss anything.

"Thank you, God, for the opportunity to share lunch with this precious family today," Jan prayed. "Thank you for the delicious food and for the hands that have prepared it. Thank you for this special day, Good Friday, when we remember the sacrifice and death of your Son. Bless and care for those who have less than us, in Jesus' name, Amen."

"Amen," everyone responded.

"Amen," I whispered, wondering what it meant.

There was a lot of chatter around the table over lunch, but my mind was processing what I'd just heard about sin, Jesus and His forgiveness.

As Mum cleared the plates, Jan looked at me intently. She was sitting directly opposite. "Would you like to invite Jesus to forgive you?" she asked.

Sitting back in my chair, I glanced at Mum. I thought about the positive change I had seen in her and the improvement in Shaz. I thought about my own life, I knew I wasn't innocent. *I need forgiveness.*

My eyes moved back towards the table, before looking back at Jan.

"How do I do that?" I asked.

"I can lead you in a prayer," she responded. "Just pray this after me."

My head dropped and I closed my eyes this time. I was concentrating and reciting every word.

"Dear God, thank you for sending your Son Jesus to die for me." I prayed. Tears were welling up from my heart. "I acknowledge I have sinned. I'm sorry for all of the wrong things I have done." I wiped my eyes trying to stop the tears dripping down my face.

"Jesus, I believe you died on the cross. I believe by God's power you rose again." I paused. My heart was pounding. "I ask you to forgive me."

I felt like all the hate and anger was pouring out of my stomach. "Come into my life and take full control," I continued. "I give my life to you today. Amen."

My head was in my hands as I sobbed and gulped for air. The tension in my shoulders had unravelled. A pool of water gathered on the table as my nose dripped like a tap. Someone placed a tissue in my hand as their arm wrapped around my shoulders.

Lifting my head, I turned to see who was comforting me. "Thank you," I whispered. The room was quiet. I swallowed a large chunk of air as a surreal peace washed over me.

Noticing the pool of water on the table I let out a chuckle. "That's embarrassing," I said, "you could swim in it."

The comment lightened the mood.

My heart was smiling as joy bubbled up inside. I felt so good. It was like a world of turmoil had ended and calm had returned.

That afternoon I sat quietly for a long time. I felt different. For years I had run on nervous energy. From the minute I got up until I went to sleep, I ran. I never sat down to read books or watch TV. Even when I sat with Shaz my mind would be in overdrive.

Something had changed. My mind had calmed. I felt relaxed. I was breathing differently. Worry had vanished.

None of it made sense. Pinching myself, I wondered if it was a dream, but it didn't go away.

I quietly whispered, "I don't know who you are God, but I know you're real. You're the answer."

***

Sunday morning, I was rummaging through my clothes rack trying to choose what to wear: *something bright, but not too loud*. "This will do," I murmured as I pulled out a purple blouse with small yellow flowers and a white skirt.

Chapter 6 | The Answer

As we were driving to church, I had butterflies in my stomach. My mind drifted back to the night I went to a local youth group with a friend.

The hall had echoed with every sound. Shoes were squeaking on the wooden floor as voices bounced in the open space. Bench seats were lined up like soldiers around the walls.

Feeling awkward I stood quietly while my friend chatted to others. My eyes glanced around the room trying to pick up what others were doing without being noticed. I fiddled with my shirt, smiling, nodding, watching. Everything within me had wanted to leave but I was stuck. *Will this church be the same?*

We turned into the church driveway. My eyes widened as I saw how many cars were parked in the grounds. Families were heading towards the entrance from all directions. People were smiling, shaking hands, and giving each other a hug.

As we approached the front door, I lifted my sunglasses. "What are you doing here?" I asked as a girl I worked with greeted me.

"I come here," she replied. "What are you doing here?"

Shrugging my shoulders, I lowered my voice and said, "I've just become a Christian."

The pitch in her voice went up a few decibels. "That's so wonderful," she said, "you'll have to tell me all about it."

Noticing people gathering I replied, "I'll catch up with you later."

The building was huge. There were rows and rows of chairs in three sections. As I followed Mum and Dad towards the middle of the left-hand side, I was greeted by a couple of people I didn't know.

Everyone stood up as the music started to play. The drummer was beating in perfect time with the music. Four singers holding microphones stepped forward on the stage.

I chuckled as I heard someone behind me clapping out of sync. The place was vibrant as people lifted their voices.

A tall man stepped on the stage as everyone sat down. "Good morning," he greeted. "Have we got any visitors here today?"

Slinking down in my chair, I looked at the floor hoping no one would notice me. Out of the corner of my eye I saw a couple across from me lift up their hands.

"Welcome" he continued. "John has a welcome pack for you. Please feel free to join us for a cuppa after the service."

Phew, they didn't see me.

He read a few announcements before inviting everyone to sing again.

After a few upbeat songs, the tempo changed. The drumming ceased. The singers stood still.

"Let's close our eyes and turn them towards Jesus," the lady on the keyboard said as she quietly played. People started to raise their hands.

The same peace I had felt two days before washed over me. The lyrics caught my heart. Tears were rolling down my cheeks, again. I felt embarrassed and nudged Mum. "Have you got a tissue?" I whispered, hoping no one would hear me.

As the song finished a lady announced the Bible reading for the day. The sound of paper crumpling caught my attention. Someone tapped my shoulder, offering me a Bible. I gave her a gentle smile wondering what to do with it. I placed it on my lap and turned my attention back to the speaker.

The words 'I will never leave you nor forsake you,' held me like they would never let go. I felt safe, secure, protected. It was a great comfort knowing the peace I had found would always be with me.

Shane, the Senior Pastor stepped onto the stage. "I will never leave you nor forsake you," he repeated as he held his Bible in the air. "What a wonderful promise. The Bible is full of wonderful promises."

I glanced down at the Bible I was clutching on my lap. *I need to get one of these. I need to learn more about God's promises. I'll have to ask Jan where I can buy one.*

He recited the story of Jesus stilling the storm from Mark Chapter 4.

Hanging on his every work, I had forgotten to breathe. *How scary that must have been for the disciples thinking they were going to drown.*

Shane started to walk back and forth on the stage. "Some of you may be facing a storm," he said.

His words reverberated in my ears. *A storm; we're facing a nightmare. But it stares back at us whenever we wake up.*

"Some of you feel like life is out of control," he continued. "It's overwhelming. You might feel like you can't keep going, like you won't make it."

My mind started racing. I felt like he was speaking directly to me. *How does he know my story? He hasn't even met me. Have Mum and Dad told him, or have Jan and Lena?*

He went back and reread the verse from Hebrews.

Taking a deep breath, I thought about Sharyn lying in the hospital bed and the story of the young guy who got healed. *If God is with us and can still a storm, can He heal Sharyn? Will He heal her?*

CHAPTER 7
The Scrap Heap

People were scurrying like ants in every direction. I did everything I could to ensure Sharyn's leg wasn't hit by anyone or anything. It didn't stop people ducking and weaving in front of us as I pushed her up the Brisbane Mall.

It was Head Injury Awareness week and Mum was doing everything she could to catch the attention of the health representative.

"Move her a bit closer," Mum said.

I cringed. *I'd rather go home.* Throngs of people were gathering. Camera crew were setting up to record the health representative's address. I inched forward.

As the health representative looked across the crowd, Mum caught his eye. "Please help me," she said, "I'm desperate. My daughter has been misplaced in the Infectious Disease Ward for two and a half years."

He took a step towards us. My whole body was shaking. *If only the ground would open up and swallow me.*

Mum didn't take her eyes off him. "Sharyn didn't meet the criteria for rehabilitation," she continued. "She needs 24/7 care and has nowhere to live."

A camera man pointed to his watch. The health representative put his hand up beckoning him to wait. He stood, calmly looking at Sharyn.

"I've written to a number of government departments," Mum continued. "Their response is always the same—a new facility will be opening soon. I've been told that for eighteen months. No government department wants to own the problem."

He looked up and summoned a team member. Mum and I both turned our heads to see a man holding a notebook walking towards us.

"I have to do an interview for Head Injury Awareness Week," he continued. "Can you give your contact details to Scott? My office will be in contact with you."

Mum's cheeks flushed as she gave me a fleeting look. *I bet she doesn't hear from them.*

A man stopped directly in front of Sharyn, perching on his tiptoes to see what was happening. I sighed. *How ignorant. How rude.* I wanted to nudge him with the wheelchair, but I refrained.

We stayed and listened to the address for a while before pushing Sharyn back down the mall.

"Would you like to support head injury?" a man called as he thrust a donation tin in front of me.

I stopped. *Are you for real? Are you blind?* My heart was racing. I looked down at Sharyn.

"I am," I responded and kept walking.

"People are so ignorant," I said to Mum as we continued down the mall. "They've got no idea. They've got no regard for people like Sharyn. They don't even see them."

A white Holden flew into the disabled park beside us as we loaded Shaz. The young girl with no sign of disability got out of the car as quickly as she had pulled in, and headed towards the lift.

Looking at Mum I shook my head. "They take their car parks too," I added. "They're a law unto themselves. It would take a tragedy in their own lives to wake them up."

***

The following evening, we were huddled around the TV. The *7:30 Report* was about to air our story. The reporter and camera crew had been to the house the previous week and visited Rose Cottage, the only facility in Brisbane caring for young people with Acquired Brain Injury.

"Dell has a desperate plea for her daughter Sharyn who suffered a traumatic head injury in a traffic accident and has nowhere to live," said the voiceover. A picture of Mum pushing Sharyn into the house was on the screen. "Sharyn has been misplaced in a hospital ward for two and a half years."

Mum's face was now in front of us. "They keep them alive only to throw them on the scrap heap," she stated.

My stomach churned as the connotation sparked an image in my mind.

"There is only one suitable facility – Rose Cottage," the reporter continued, "however, there's an eight-year waiting list." Pictures of the cream walls, the large lounge chairs and long tables were shown.

"Look at those curtains," I remarked. "They're awful."

"Shhh," Mum said as she motioned with her hand.

"There's only been one vacancy in the last two and a half years," the reporter continued.

"Oh no," I said as a photo of me sitting with Sharyn came on the screen. "I didn't know they were filming me. I can't believe I wore that shirt. Look at my hair."

The phone rang constantly that night.

"We saw your story on the TV."

"How's Sharyn's going?"

"Is there anything we can do to help?"

***

My last appointment the following day was close to home. I skipped towards the car. *I'll get an early mark today, woohoo.* The house was quiet when I arrived home. I arranged a few reports and a cup of tea on the side table and pulled the lever to lift my legs.

The phone rang.

Not again. It will have to go to the answering machine.

Brrring, brrring!

A piercing stare came from Mum as she lifted the receiver. *Where did you come from? I didn't know you were home.*

She stood holding the phone. Her eyes looked serious; her lips pursed. She was nodding.

I sighed as I sat upright. *Has something happened to Shaz?*

Mum finally spoke. "That's wonderful," she replied. Her shoulders relaxed as she put down the receiver.

"They're giving Sharyn a respite bed for six weeks at Rose Cottage, starting Monday," Mum said. "The government representative has promised she won't have to go back to the Infectious Disease Ward."

Marvelling at how strong Mum was, I gave her a tight hug. "You've fought for so long," I said, "It's all paid off."

She stood seemingly unchanged, calmly smiling back at me.

My eyebrows furrowed as I scrunched my nose. "Where are they going to put her after the six weeks?" I asked.

Mum shrugged. "I'm not sure," she replied. "We can't relax. We're one step in the right direction though. We can only go forward."

***

Sharyn's few belongings were packed up in a box. My emotions were mixed. We had met some wonderful people who we knew we wouldn't see again. A tear escaped as we farewelled Sharyn's favourite hairdresser.

"We're never coming back here," I said as we drove down the hill. "Thankfully."

With gentle music playing in the van my thoughts celebrated how far we'd come. *With help we purchased the van, Mum negotiated getting Sharyn home, we met Jan and Lena, and now we've got respite.*

"Thank you, God," I whispered. "You're always with us."

"How much easier is this?" Mum said as she turned into the entrance of Rose Cottage. "I don't need help to park here."

"Hello, Sharyn," the nurse unit manager greeted as she bent down to eye level. "It's lovely to see you."

Mum and I exchanged a smile.

Chapter 7 | The Scrap Heap

My fingers nervously tapped the handles on Sharyn's chair as we followed her into the building. *Mum was right; we're not the only family suffering.*

"You look good today," one of the patients said as he wheeled his chair towards me. His deep blue eyes radiating joy.

"Thank you," I replied. "What's your name?"

"Tim," he replied.

"Hello Tim," I said. "It's nice to meet you."

A few minutes later he repeated the same words.

My mind twitched as I looked back at him with a smile. "Thank you," I replied the second time realising his head injury must have impacted his short-term memory.

A cup dropping on the floor startled me. I turned to see a carer coming to a young girl's aid. My eyes shifted quickly so as not to embarrass her.

"It will be good for Shaz to have a place where she's with others," I said to Mum as we entered her room. "At least there'll be some activity and interaction."

Mum placed a few things in the drawer. "You won't be on your own at night, Shaz," I said as I drew the curtain. The other end seemed to follow me around the track. "You've got a little garden outside, too."

"I'm going to find someone to hook Sharyn's peg feed up," Mum said. "Do you want to bring Sharyn out into the common area?"

The mere thought of it overwhelmed me. The hospital was all we had known for two and a half years. We were now in a new place filled with young people whose lives had been broken, just like Shaz.

"We'll have to brave it sometime," I murmured to Shaz as I turned her wheelchair around. "Let's go."

Bingo balls were rattling like a mouse on a wheel as a staff member turned the cage. My eyes scanned the room looking for somewhere to sit.

"Here we go, Shaz," I said quietly as a cream chair caught my eye. "Let's go over near the window."

I sat discreetly observing the residents. Some were lying in large lounge chairs on wheels, unable to move. Others were wheeling themselves around looking for someone to talk to. Feelings of sadness overwhelmed me as the cruelty of life glared at me.

"Ny, this is Karen," Mum said. "Karen's going to look after Shaz this afternoon."

The thought of leaving Shaz with people who didn't know her worried me. *She's so vulnerable not being able to speak. How are they going to know what she needs? There are copious notes but who'd have time to read them?*

The lump in my throat was remerging. "We'll be back tonight, Shaz," I whispered as I stroked her arm. My heart sank as we walked out.

Sharyn was calmer and more settled after the transition. We all were.

She had only been at Rose Cottage three weeks when Mum secretly beckoned me into her room.

"I want to show you something."

CHAPTER 8
One Thousand Brains

I couldn't blink. My heart was pounding as I stood poised with my finger. *What if she chokes?*

Mum had broken off a tiny piece of chocolate and placed it under Sharyn's tongue.

I was in awe as I watched Sharyn thrust it onto the roof of her mouth with her tongue and continue to suck it.

"How long have you been sneaking that?" I asked.

"A couple of weeks," Mum replied with a cheeky grin. "I believe she'll be able to eat eventually."

My eyes widened as I shook my head. "You never give up, do you? You're amazing."

Mum's persistence and determination had lifted Sharyn over a number of hurdles, but it sometimes took its toll. As the weeks in respite ticked, her eyes grew sadder. Her energy levels had dropped as she dragged one foot after the other.

"Can you please consider turning the respite bed Sharyn is presently using at Rose Cottage into a permanent bed?" Mum pleaded with the chief executive officer on the phone. "Sharyn has been allocated a bed at Daisy Lodge, but it is on the other side of town. The daily travelling and tolls are going to increase financial pressure on the family and it will take Sharyn away from all of her established support and therapy."

Her eyes had lost their sparkle. Hope had turned to despair. She had done everything in her power to keep Sharyn close to the family home, but it had made no difference.

"Why don't we go and have a look at Daisy Lodge?" Dad said. "We'll time how long it takes to get there."

As we drove down the road, I put my foot on the brakes. "There's the hospital," I said as I pointed to the sign. "It must be the next driveway."

The small building was tucked away at the bottom of a long cement road surrounded by freshly mown grass and nestled amongst trees well advanced in years.

The clear air filled my nostrils as I stepped out of the car. "You wouldn't even know it's here," I whispered as we peered through the lattice.

Mum was looking at the garden at the side of the large patio. "What a beautiful area," she replied. "Shaz will love sitting out here."

"It's nice and secure too," Dad added.

"Let's have a look around the back," I said as I darted around the corner. A small lizard slid under crumpled leaves. Observing the bushland behind the building, I could hear a Kookaburra laughing in the distance. *This is so calm and private.*

Mum released a huge sigh as she stood staring back up the path. "It's next door to the hospital, too, if anything goes wrong."

I relaxed when I heard those words.

***

Sharyn's move to Daisy Lodge was only a week away. Mum, Dad and I were sitting in the pergola area waiting to meet the nurse unit manager. Mum was unwrapping a chocolate.

"Any for me?" I asked as I looked up with a pleading gaze. She moved the container towards me.

"Here she is," Mum said as she saw the door open at the top of the stairs.

Chapter 8 | One Thousand Brains

My muscles tensed. Andrea the nurse unit manager's stance and eye contact unnerved me. I stood in Dad's shadow as we were greeted.

Her thin build didn't match her strength or tone of voice as she passionately talked about the services. I quickly looked away whenever her gaze turned towards me.

I couldn't get to the car quick enough. "What is it with that lady?" I asked as we drove off. "She's scary."

"You'll get used to her," Mum replied. "She's a wonderful advocate for Acquired Brain Injury and driven to get the best for young people like Shaz. She may be a bit intimidating, but she's kind at heart."

"I wouldn't want to get on the wrong side of her," I responded.

***

Sharyn was the second resident to enter Daisy Lodge. The staff were warm and friendly and went out of their way to try to understand Sharyn and her needs.

One by one the beds were filled. We sat at a distance, knowing every family had suffered a similar fate. Instinctively, we'd look out for each other's loved one.

"You've got a thousand brains in your head," one of Sharyn's roommates said as I walked in. My heart smiled.

"How are you today?" I responded, giving her arm a little pat as she lay in her bed.

She cackled.

"What have you girls been up to today?" I asked.

"F--- off!" one of the girls screeched. I gulped. *Oops, too close, too loud.* I quickly retreated to the chair next to Shaz. She continued to hover. I decided not to maintain eye contact or ask any further questions.

I pulled out the magazine to hide a little and read to Shaz. As I sat quietly, I could hear the oxygen concentrator rattling from across the room. I looked over to see the other resident lying with her mask on.

"I'll pop over and say hi, once our friend here moves," I whispered to Shaz. "I don't want to disturb her."

As the weeks passed, I slowly warmed to Andrea. She worked hard with staff to develop first class care in a flexible and homelike environment. Normalisation and socialisation underpinned everything they did.

We relaxed more and more as Sharyn gained access to therapy and the community. The fight for a suitable place to live was over, even though it was on the other side of town.

***

I hid my eyes in my hands as the recreational officer invited me to attend one of their outings with Sharyn and other residents. "You can't do that," I said as I scrambled to find other words.

The thought of bounding into an all you can eat restaurant with ten young people in wheelchairs was mind bending.

"They'll overtake the restaurant," I continued. "What about the other people dining there? It will be so imposing."

"Just come," she replied. "You don't have to do anything. I'll look after Sharyn. Just come."

I slowly moved my hands back.

***

I was feeling light-headed and nauseous the day of the outing. My eyes were darting back and forth trying to calculate how many people would be at the restaurant as the bus pulled into the carpark.

Staff assisted the residents one by one. A few heads turned as furniture was shifted to make room for the wheelchairs. Most smiled and returned back to their conversations. My mind settled as my fears of imposing on other diners dissipated.

The smiles on the resident's faces brightened the room like a field full of sunflowers. Staff caringly helped those who were able to choose what they wanted from the buffet.

My anxiety turned to joy as the atmosphere of bantering and laughter filled the air. "Thank you," I said to the recreational officer as we moved back towards the bus. "You've helped me overcome a huge hurdle today. I can't thank you enough."

Her cheeky look told me she was just getting started.

Chapter 8 | One Thousand Brains

As we pulled back into the driveway, I noticed one of the other resident's parents walking towards the unit. Her face was pale and pained.

"I thought you were going on a holiday," I said as I approached her.

She recoiled, sheltering her arm.

"What happened?" I asked.

"I was downtown a few days ago," she replied. "I fell as I got out of the car and fractured my shoulder."

Smack!

My heart pounded as the injustice hit me in the stomach. My fists and teeth were clenched "That's so unfair!" I shouted. "If anyone deserves a holiday you do. Why can't anything go right?"

Her son had suffered a head injury in a traffic accident. Over time, with the support of her husband, they had nursed him back to health. Despite having some vision impairment, his licence had been reinstated. It wasn't long before he had another accident, leaving him completely disabled.

"Well, dear," she said in a quiet, calm tone. "When I fell, there was a doctor passing. He helped me and called an ambulance."

As I took a breath, I inhaled the peace that was oozing out of her.

"When I was in excruciating pain at the hospital," she continued, "a nurse would sit with me and rub my arm."

I stood staring at her as her gratitude flowed like a river after the rain. *How can you be so positive and thankful at a time like this? You've been through so much. I'd be so mad. I am mad.*

My thoughts overwhelmed me as I realised, she had something I hadn't found. She had an acceptance for anything that came her way.

I didn't. I fought against Sharyn's condition. I wanted our lives to change. I wanted Sharyn to get healed so we could go back to normal. Acceptance wasn't in me.

Life itself grieved me. *Sharyn has lost everything. We've lost everything. It all seems so unfair. It is unfair.*

***

A few days later I caught up with a friend for a walk along the waterfront. I was almost jogging to keep up with her walking pace.

"What happened to Shaz?" she asked tentatively.

I paused as I looked out across the sea of blue water mirroring the sky. "Sharyn was travelling down to visit me with a friend, who was relocating for work," I replied. "She thought it was a good idea to introduce us so that he had a contact in Sydney."

"She was going to spend the weekend with me before flying home," I continued. My words caught in my throat. "They failed to give way at an intersection in Armidale and collided with a truck."

My friend's walking pace slowed. "Was Sharyn driving?" she asked.

My lips pressed tight as I closed my eyes. "No, her friend was," I replied.

"What happened to him?" she continued.

I held my breath for longer than usual before blurting. "He had a broken collarbone."

The conversation turned as a beautiful white Labrador nudged towards us on the path.

***

Later that week, I was having lunch with a friend when the story came up, again.

"What happened to the driver?" she asked. My response was the same, a delayed breath followed by a splurt of words.

"Do you blame him?" she continued.

I shook my head. "It was an accident," I reasoned. "We all make mistakes on the road. It could have been any one of us."

As I drove home, my reaction was staring back at me like I was looking in the mirror. My thoughts arrested me. *Why do you hold your breath so tight before you answer that question? If you didn't blame him, you would say, 'Thank God he was okay.'*

The revelation was like removing a band aid from a festering sore. Suppressed anger and resentment had oozed its way to the surface. My tears were flooding like a dam wall that had just been released.

I pulled off the road as my body shook uncontrollably. "God, please forgive me," I prayed. "Forgive him. Please release him from any burden of guilt. Release me."

Cars whizzed by as I sat quietly regaining my composure. As I drove home, I realised changes were happening every day. I was becoming a different person. Things were looking brighter.

CHAPTER 9
Turned Around

Six months prior to Sharyn's accident I had started a job I didn't think was possible.

Mum had arrived home from work with excitement in her eyes. "I've got something for you," she said as she placed the flyer on the table. "You might like this."

After looking at it for a few minutes I glanced back at her. "Did you read the criteria?" I questioned as I raised the flyer in the air. I didn't wait for the answer. "They're looking for someone with a Senior Certificate and tertiary education."

"I definitely don't fit the criteria," I murmured. "I've only done Junior and six months at TAFE. Have you gone mad?"

"It doesn't cost you anything to apply," she replied as she headed into the kitchen.

Puffing a bit of air out of my lips, I rolled my eyes, and placed it back on the table.

A few days later I picked the flyer up again. *A Cadetship in Travel Consultancy. Mum's right, I've got nothing to lose and it will be a way out of where I am.*

I sat in disbelief when I received a phone call. "There'll be a two-part interview," the receptionist said. "The first part will require you to name places in Queensland on a map. Part two will be a face-to-face interview."

Places in Queensland. My mind was spinning. *I wouldn't have a clue. I've travelled Europe but I know nothing about Queensland. I've lived here all my life but I've only been to the Gold and Sunshine Coast and Roma for holidays.*

Sharyn was working for an Insurance company in the city and was my only hope.

"Can you go to the nearest travel agent in your lunch hour and pick up every brochure you can on Queensland?" I pleaded.

That evening and the following day I tried to memorise towns inland and along the Queensland coastline. Not confident I would remember all of them and fearful my nerves would get the better of me, I slipped a map into my handbag.

"Take your time," the receptionist said as she handed me the clipboard. "You've got half an hour before the interview."

Placing my handbag on the table, I sat down in the small waiting room. I managed to get a number of the towns listed, but there were still a few blank dots.

I didn't dare to look up as my darting eyes would easily give me away. Mustering up a fake sneeze, I slowly looked into the handbag for a tissue. The glimpse of the map was enough to prompt me with what I needed. I quietly blew my nose, paused for a few minutes and went back to the clipboard. Part one was over.

The interview must have gone okay as I was offered the cadetship in Sydney. Two of us were appointed. One was to work in the city office and the other in Parramatta. We would then change over halfway through the cadetship.

***

The day I started; a young man bounded into the office. He was full of enthusiasm and changed the atmosphere of the room. Everyone seemed delighted to see him.

Chapter 9 | Turned Around

I leant forward towards the girl sitting beside me and took off my phone headset. "Who's that?" I asked.

"He's the Sydney sales representative," she replied. "He's got the best job. He travels around and promotes all of our new holiday packages with travel agents. He also takes them on trips to Queensland to familiarise them with some of the hotels and activities we promote."

I looked over to see where he was. He was sitting on one of the workers desks having a chat. "That's what I want to do," I whispered, "when I've gained some experience."

My dream died the day Sharyn had her accident. Everything did.

A new role was created in the Brisbane wholesale department making way for me to return home and finish my cadetship.

The work wasn't stimulating. I missed the face to face contact with clients helping them to create their holidays. I keyed in at 09:00am and keyed out at 5:00pm.

Having less responsibility gave me more time to help with Shaz, but I was bored. I trudged along putting my best foot forward, but I was tired, empty, and void of any hope.

Darkness had crept in. Everything seemed shallow and meaningless. I had no energy or desire to go out or maintain friendships. How could I when Sharyn couldn't even lift her head? I had lost my smile.

Eighteen months after Sharyn's accident, the fire was reignited when the sales representative position in Brisbane became vacant. *This is it. I can't believe it. I've wanted to do this for so long.*

I submitted my application and waited expectantly every day for a phone call. Days turned into a week. My hope started to fade as my mind wreaked havoc. *Maybe it's because of Shaz. Maybe they don't think I have the capacity.*

The flame was put out as quickly as it had started when I received the thank you but no thank you letter.

I was devastated.

Rhianna worked in our department. She couldn't stop talking about her excitement when she found out she got the job.

"Congratulations," I said to her, smiling behind gritted teeth. "You're going to love it. I'm so excited for you." Deep down I was seething. *It should have been me. I've been here longer than her. Why couldn't it have been me?*

Life was hard, but I was finding the same determination I had seen in Mum so many times. I wasn't going to give up. *This is where I want to be in the organisation. If I can't get there, I'm going to have to leave the company to gain further experience.*

***

Moving to an inbound tour company, I expanded my skills creating itineraries for people travelling to Australia from overseas. I enjoyed the work but it wasn't my dream job.

Rhianna was only in the job twelve months when she resigned.

Calling the organisation to following up on my group certificate I heard the news. *I need to ring Jerry.*

"I hear you're looking for a sales representative," I said when Jerry answered the phone.

"Gee word travels fast," he replied. "Are you interested?"

A smile stretched across my face as I responded. "I certainly am."

"The job will be advertised tomorrow," he said. "I look forward to seeing your application."

I couldn't contain my excitement. *I'm not waiting. I'm going to show you how much I want this job. You'll be seeing me tomorrow.*

The following day I was at the office bright and early.

"Is Jerry in?" I asked as I stood at the reception desk.

The receptionist gave me a knowing smile as she picked up the phone and pressed the three digits to his extension.

"Hi Jerry, I've got Nyree at reception." She put the phone down. "He'll be out in a minute."

"That was quick," he said as he walked down the hallway.

Jerry always had a cheerful disposition and a great sense of humour. Just seeing him made me happy.

"I was in the area so I thought I would deliver my application."

Chapter 9 | Turned Around

He gave me a cheeky look. "We'll be in touch."

The following Wednesday I received a call from Human Resources. "Would you be free for an interview on Friday at 10:00am?"

My heart was pounding as I tried to find my voice. "Yes, I am," I replied. My legs were kicking under the desk. *I'm so excited.*

That night I listed all the positives about the organisation and looked over the current brochures trying to memorise some of the holiday specials. I finished with a list of why I was the best person for the job.

The smile never left my face as I travelled to the office.

Fidgeting with a rubber band, I sat in the waiting room reciting my words. *I've worked in both the retail and the wholesale departments for over two years. My understanding of how to coordinate itineraries had increased in my current job.*

A chuckle emerged as I remembered slipping the map of Queensland into my bag three years earlier.

"Nyree," the receptionist called. "You can go in."

As I walked around the corner Jerry stood up to greet me. He was still wearing his cheeky smile.

We chatted about a number of things happening in the news, the latest gadgets on the market, and the organisation's main competitor in the industry.

Feeling deflated I headed back to the lift. *Is that it? He didn't even ask me why I'd be the best person for the job.*

I tried to be positive but my heart got heavier as my fears continued to boomerang. *I don't want to miss out, again.*

Excitement re-emerged when I was offered the second interview a few days later.

My fingers were rubbing the strap of my handbag as I walked nervously towards the CEO.

"You've got some great references here," he said as he looked up from the desk.

"Thanks," I replied. "I paid good money for them."

My mind spluttered. *Where did that come from?*

He laughed as he encouraged me to take a seat.

The flippant comment of paying for my references had slipped out. *I hop it doesn't go against me.*

CHAPTER 10

My hands were trembling with excitement as I removed my headset and jumped up and down. Heads were bobbing around the petitions wondering what the commotion was.

"I got the job!" I shouted. "My dream job, and it's close to home."

Sharyn had settled in Daisy Lodge. The heavy weight on Mum and Dad's shoulders had eased and new opportunities were opening up for me. I could travel and be home regularly.

A month later I was on my first trip leading a group of travel agents to the Whitsundays to familiarise them with some of the holiday destinations.

The bus was at the entrance of the obscure little coastal airport in Proserpine ready to take us to the first resort.

I was checking my watch every five minutes. The manager wasn't in any hurry. The travel agents had looked through the resort and were gathered around a table lined with champagne, cheese, and tropical fruit platters.

Wiggling my toes, I wondered how we were going to get out of there to get to the next one.

"We're running half an hour late," I said as I called the second manager. "We'll be there at 3:30pm."

As we arrived at our last hotel, we had free time before gathering for dinner. The cabins were nestled individually in front of towering palm trees. I sat on the small patio watching the birds flitting between trees.

"You're a bit lovely," I said to the Lorikeet as it landed on the railing. "Are you looking for food?" His little head twitched before flying to his next destination. A tinge of sadness pinged my heart as I sat in the tranquillity thinking about how Shaz was unable to get outside without someone taking her. *She would love it here.*

Dinner was noisier than a large family gathering. Jokes were flying as we sat gathered around long wooden tables under the twinkling stars. It got louder as the night went on. The hotel was doing everything to create a memorable experience. Drinks were poured in abundance as the travel agents served themselves from the buffet.

They were like birds let out of a cage.

"Let's go in here," one of them said as we wandered through town that evening.

Everyone filed into the pub jammed with backpackers and loud music.

"Breakfast is at 6:00am tomorrow," I declared to the agents as I prepared to head back to the hotel. "The bus will be leaving at 7:00am, sharp."

I chuckled as a number of them staggered to breakfast. "Late night, hey?" I said as I noticed bloodshot eyes. "What time did you get back?"

A number of heads dropped. "Three o'clock," one of them replied, as a smirk crossed his face. "We were having too much fun."

Munching on my warm croissant smeared with butter, I discreetly did a head count and noticed one of the agents was missing. *The guys are all here. It must be one of the girls.* I ran my finger down the manifest.

"Has anyone seen Melissa this morning" I asked.

Heads were shaking.

"She came back with us last night," one of the guys responded. "She wasn't in very good shape."

"I'll go and check on her," one of the girls said. "What room is she in?"

"208," I replied. "Can you let her know the bus is leaving in half an hour."

Chapter 10 | Crossaints

Melissa emerged ten minutes later. She was slightly hunched over, her sunglasses covering her eyes and the colour sapped from her face.

"Morning," I said as I raised my eyebrows. "How are we today?"

She gave me a fleeting smile as she headed towards the coffee machine. A round of applause rose from the table.

"Go away," she said, as she signalled with her hand.

As we arrived at the Airlie Beach Marina, I led the agents down the jetty towards the sleek, white, Hayman Island cruiser. We were greeted by four staff with beaming smiles. They looked immaculate. You couldn't see a wrinkle on their white shirts or their faces for that matter.

"Welcome aboard," John said with an outstretched arm. "Please make your way inside the cabin for a briefing and light refreshments before we disembark."

I waited as the agents stepped onto the boat. I numbered them off one by one making sure Melissa was still with us. The interior was just as grandiose as the outside. I could see my reflection in the meticulously clean tables, surrounded by luxurious seating.

"I can't believe I get paid to do this," I said, as we sat in the hot tropical weather gliding over the rich, blue water. "I've got the best job in the world."

"You better watch your back," one of the agents replied.

The secluded piece of paradise was nestled in front of mountainous cliffs wrapping themselves around the whole resort. The diamond shaped pool twinkled as it made its way just short of the ocean. Beach umbrellas shaded chairs scattered along its edge.

"Wow," one of the agents said as she entered the room. "This is extravagant. I can't believe we get to stay here."

After lunch we boarded the seaplane bound for Whitehaven beach.

"Are you okay?" I asked Melissa as she stood at a distance.

"I'm nervous about the plane," she said sheepishly. "It's pretty small."

"It's the first time I've been on one too," I replied. "You can sit with me. We'll brave it together."

The expanse of the reef and the swirling sand displays in the turquoise water were breathtaking from the air. I turned to comment to Melissa and noticed her face was whiter than the silicon sand below.

Quickly reaching for a sick bag, I gagged, trying to keep myself from hurling as she poured her lunch into it.

"The perks of the job, hey?" I heard someone whisper from behind as they tapped me on the shoulder.

I chuckled as I tried to disengage my mind from the bag I was holding.

The pilot passed a plastic bag which secured it until we landed.

Gathering in as much fresh air as my lungs would hold, I stepped out of the plane. The odour lingering in my nostrils slowly discharged.

As we walked along the beach the exceptionally fine and impeccably white sand felt like silk under my feet. The crystal-clear water washed the residue from my mind. *I'll have to make a note about Melissa for future reference.*

***

After months of meeting with travel agents across Brisbane I flew to Cairns. I had a week to travel back to Gladstone where I was roped into doing a bird man jump at their festival.

"We've put you on the 10th floor tonight Miss Mannion," the receptionist said as she handed me the key. "Enjoy your stay."

As I opened the door the view took my breath away. The sky was a myriad of red, orange, and yellow as the sun disappeared behind the mountains. The water was glistening as clouds dispersed across the sky. I picked up the camera. *The reports will have to wait.*

I dialled 2 for room service and sat on the balcony, watching the mountains disappear as the night sky overtook them. The sound of cars and chatter from the restaurants below filled the air.

Scanning the figures, highlighting agencies whose sales had increased and decreased, I could see it had been a good quarter. I thanked God for the wonderful opportunity he had given me, prayed for Shaz, and turned out the light.

Chapter 10 | Crossaints

The following morning, I picked up the fresh croissants I had ordered from the hotel and headed to my first appointment.

The week was busy visiting agents and coordinating future familiarisations. Every night was different as I moved from five-star hotels to three-star resorts, trialling their restaurants and experiencing their hospitality.

I pulled into Gladstone just in time to visit our agents before closing time.

Des' eyes were jumping as he produced the birdman outfit.

"Will I flop or fly?" I asked as he placed the halo on my head. The white angel wings stood as tall as me displaying our logo on both sides.

Des chuckled as he took a photo.

The four-metre platform above the river glared at me as we entered the car park the following morning. People were wrapping, taping and climbing into all sorts of contraptions.

"The things I do for promotion," I said. "I must be crazy."

Heavenly jokes were flying as staff from the office affixed my wings with masking tape.

I nearly toppled as I stepped forward. "There's got to be an easier way to get there," I joked. "I'm not sure I'm ready."

The laughter was contagious as I tried to shuffle towards the barge which would ferry me across the river to the scaffolding.

"How on earth am I going to get up there?" I asked as we approached the twenty steps leading to the platform. "Whose idea was this?"

One of the security divers floating in the river called out. "Can you get out of your equipment easily?"

My body was shaking more than my lips. "I hope so," I shouted nervously as I looked down towards the water.

My palms were sweating. *What if I can't get out?*

"You're up." Des called.

I started to run. My scream bellowed through the air as I plummeted straight down and hit the water in less than two seconds. I refilled my lungs as soon as I realised I was floating on top of the river.

Adrenalin was rushing through my body. I couldn't stop smiling as they ferried me to shore. Everyone gathered around.

"Well done," they said as they recited how loud I screamed.

"Flying is fun," I replied. "Even if it's just for a split second." My excitement plummeted as I hopped in the car to return to Brisbane. *If only Shaz was free to spread her wings.*

It was more than Sharyn's needs that led me to fly in a different direction eighteen months later.

CHAPTER 11
No Room

As I picked up the sticky note on my desk, I looked around the room. *Am I in trouble? What have I done?* My mind was filtering through the events of the previous few weeks. Nothing jumped out. *Has someone complained?*

I walked slowly towards Jerry's office.

The view always caught my breath as the sky and the river spread in all directions.

"Have a seat," Jerry said.

My hands were clasped, my back straight, my shoe tapping the floor. A strange gadget on the desk caught my eye. *Don't ask, I reminded myself. You may never get out of here.*

I remembered the time I had asked about the palm pilot. Jerry sat showing me how it organised his calendar. Every entry prompted another story. He then demonstrated how it stored his contacts. I eventually left forgetting to ask my question. I couldn't bring myself to go back in.

"We've been putting a plan together," Jerry said.

As his words hit my ears I relaxed. *Phew. I'm not in trouble.* I moved back in my chair, placed my fingers on the desk and stretched my toes.

"We want to do a sales blitz next year," he continued. "Probably early March."

I turned my head slightly to watch the CityCat glide under the story bridge.

"We want to send all the sales reps to Sydney, Melbourne, Adelaide, Perth, Canberra and New Zealand."

I looked back at him with wide eyes as my ears pricked.

"We'll give you a week in each capital and two weeks in NZ," he continued.

"That sounds amazing," I said as I clapped my hands. "Will they be coming to Queensland?"

"We'll bring them to Queensland later in the year," he replied.

The intrigue got the better of me. "What's this?" I asked as I pointed to the gadget on the desk. *Dammit.*

"It's an audio recorder," he responded as his eyes danced. "You can record audio and speed the vocals up or slow them down. It was Macaulay Culkin's favourite toy in Home Alone 2. The boys have been pestering Deidre and I for one for months. We've bought it for them for Christmas."

"They'll love it," I responded with a chuckle. "You better watch what you say around the house."

My thoughts were clambering as I strolled towards the Botanic Gardens for lunch. *It's going to be a lot of work. Six weeks is a long time on the road. Things will be busier when I get back. What about Shaz? I'm usually only away for a week at a time.*

"Are you looking for money?" I heard a voice call from behind.

Turning around I noticed a work colleague, Craig, standing with raised eyebrows.

"Someone once told me people who walk with their head down are looking for money," he continued.

"No," I replied as I chuckled. "I'm just deep in thought."

"Have you got time for a drink?" he asked.

"If you're paying," I responded with a nudge.

Chapter 11 | No Room

We sat on the edge of a long wooden bench. "What are you having?" he asked as he pulled his wallet from his back pocket.

"I'll have a cappuccino, thanks," I responded, throwing a smile.

"Any food?"

I shook my head as I lifted my takeaway container from my bag. I sat fiddling with a packet of sugar as I watched people passing by the river glistening in the sun. I leant back putting my fingers through my hair.

"I heard you topped the sales nationally this year," Craig said as he hoisted his right leg over the seat.

Putting my thumbs in the air, I winked. "The agents in Gladstone had a lot to do with it," I replied. "Their sales have been through the roof. The miners head to the coast for fresh air and sunlight whenever they're off duty."

The noise of jet skiers going full throttle down the river caught our attention. "That looks like so much fun," I said, as I sipped my coffee.

"Jerry gave me three nights on Orpheus Island, as a reward," I continued.

"Are you kidding me?" he asked as his eyes widened. "What's it like?"

Rubbing my fingers on my forehead, I spoke slowly, lowering my voice. "It is an unspoilt tropical paradise," I replied, before letting silence linger. I leant forward. "It's so secluded," I continued. "They have a maximum of twenty-eight people on the island at any time."

His Adam's Apple was bobbing up and down. "As you step out of your room the turquoise water is footsteps away. The only noises are birds chirping, water lapping and the sound of your own breath."

I could smell his breath.

As I put my cup back on the table he looked up. "Did you take anyone with you?" he asked.

I placed my hand over my mouth as I nodded. "Yes," I replied. "I took Mum."

We both laughed.

"We had a great time."

"I've got to get back to work," I said as I picked up my bag.

"Yeah, me too," he replied. "Thanks for the coffee."

As I drove home that evening, my thoughts were blaring. *You're going to have to work twice as hard in the lead up. Your work's going to pile up and your sales will drop.*

I turned the music up a couple of notches. *It's not until March. I'll have plenty of time to prepare.*

My thoughts were still blasting as I arrived home. *You'll be with people all the time; breakfast, lunch and dinner. There'll be no room. What about Shaz? Is it time to leave?*

The smell of home cooked food gave me a small reprieve as I opened the front door. It was fleeting. The volume in my head got louder.

Picking up a notebook I ruled a line down the centre of the page. My brain was moving faster than my hand could write as I listed the pros and cons of staying or going.

"Do you want some dinner?" Mum called from the top of the stairs.

"I'll be up in a minute," I replied as the uneven list stared back at me.

"How's your day?" Mum asked as she placed the noodles into the dish.

"I saw Craig," I replied.

"Oh…and?" she responded. The air was silent for a moment.

My face blushing. "He bought me a coffee," I replied.

"How was your day?" I asked, flicking the ball back to her side of the court.

"Nothing out of the ordinary," she replied. "I went and saw Shaz and then got my hair cut. Leanne was telling me about a Bible College her Dad was going to."

"You should think about Bible College," she continued.

My mouthful of chicken nearly ended up across the table. Parts of it went up my nose. I ran to spit the remaining pieces into a tissue. I sat back down, but couldn't hold it together. I started to laugh. It was hurting. I had to bend over to catch some breath. My face was going red. I couldn't stop. Mum was now laughing. It was contagious.

Chapter 11 | No Room

The pressure of the day had burst. I relaxed. *I think I'll give the decision about my job more time.*

***

Every day my thoughts tossed back and forth like a ball in a tennis match. *Queensland is manageable, but six weeks in other states? It's a long time to be away. It's only for a season. I'll just need to work harder.*

I could leave and get a part time job. It would give me time to bring Shaz home on other days. We could listen to preaching and learn more about God. There'll be no time for that on the road with sales reps and travel agents morning, noon and night. I have the best job in the world. I'd be crazy to leave. The inner turmoil sapped my energy.

My heart got heavier as Christmas approached. Celebrating was always hard after Sharyn's accident. We attended the morning church service before collecting Shaz. Jan and Lena arrived not long after us.

Jan's eyes were sparkling as I shared the many stories of how God had provided for us. Her smile never left her face.

"You should consider going to Bible College," Jan said as I came up for air. "There's a great one not far from here."

I glanced at Mum as my mind thought about the chicken going up my nose a couple of weeks earlier. *How weird, this has come up again.*

"I've got a sales blitz coming up next year," I said, diverting the conversation.

Nothing more was said about the college, but it sparked curiosity in me. *I wonder what they do there? I didn't know such a thing existed.*

Entering the New Year I had a decision to make. Time had run out. I couldn't hold on any longer. I knew what I needed to do. I just needed to take the step.

CHAPTER 12

Four Hours

Jerry's face went pale. The room was silent.

I pursed my lips trying to hold back the tears. My eyes were blinking incessantly. I waited.

He sat staring at my letter of resignation. He eventually looked up. His head tilted to the side, looking at me incredulously.

"What's happened?" he asked in a quiet tone.

My head turned away as I tried to find my words. "I've decided to go to Bible College," I responded.

He was google-eyed.

"You!" he said as he pointed towards me. "You're going to Bible College?"

The shift in the atmosphere came instantaneously.

Jerry slapped the table and doubled over with mirth.

"Are you going to sit in a room for an hour and not speak?" he taunted.

I tried to throw back a strong look of disapproval but a smirk broke before I could find it. My voice bubbled.

"I'm going to try."

He couldn't contain his laughter.

"Oh, how I'd love to be a fly on the wall," he said as he folded his arms.

I thought the decision would bring peace, but I was restless. I sat at my desk well after everyone had gone home. *How am I going to tell everyone? No one even knows I'm a Christian. The way news travels they'll have me becoming a Catholic nun heading to a monastery in no time.*

My thoughts were echoing in the silence of the office. The whirring from the computer room seemed to be in sync with the fan above. An eerie darkness crept from the surrounding offices shut down for the long weekend.

A flicker of light came from the computer screen inspiring me to send an email. *Great idea. Everyone will get the same information at the same time.*

My fingers were crawling like spiders' legs as I tapped the keyboard. As I wrote about Sharyn's accident, pain gripped my throat. I couldn't breathe. Once the first tear broke free, the rest followed in an unbroken stream.

Walking around the office I was trying to overcome the gouging within. An image of the disciples drowning in the storm flashed into my mind. "Jesus, you're with me," I whispered. "Please help me."

As the peace I had come to know so well settled my heart, I sat back down. *I need to be bold and share my story. Others need to know I believe in God and believe He can heal Sharyn. They need the same opportunity to pray as I have done to invite Jesus into my life.*

My finger hovered over the send button like a plane waiting to land as I read the four pages over and over. I looked up. *It's now or never.*

***

Monday afternoon I was pacing. *What are staff going to say tomorrow? Am I going to get strange looks when I arrive at the office? Will they curse me?*

I whispered another prayer. "Please God, help them to believe."

Everything seemed normal as I entered the office. There were no stares or sniggers.

As I opened my emails a message from the CEO was glaring at me. 'Work emails are for office use only.'

Chapter 12 | FOUR HOURS

I dropped my head as my eyes darted.

Oops.

Sorry.

Too late.

The usual quiet lunchroom was buzzing with chatter. "Do you believe in God?" a staff member asked another.

"I've never really thought about God," came the reply.

I skipped out of the room, excited to hear God's name being mentioned in a positive way not just blasphemously.

My final month provided many opportunities to share my journey before handing back my keys.

"It's been the best job I've ever had," I said to Jerry as he placed the keys on his desk. My eyes were twinkling, my smile broadening. "Do you want to know something?" I asked.

He shrugged as he glanced at the clock.

"When I went for my interview for the cadetship, I cheated."

His eyes widened as he stood motionless.

"I didn't know much about Queensland, so I snuck a map into my bag."

Elevating his eyebrows, he let out a chuckle. "You didn't?"

I snorted as I drew back some breath. "I did," I replied. "It was my only hope of remembering all of the towns."

He rubbed his eyes in disbelief. "Well you've been a great rep," he replied. "Don't be a stranger."

"I'll think of you every time I see a fly on the wall," I responded. "Thanks, for everything."

***

The following week I was sitting at my desk staring at the book we were required to read before starting college.

Picking up the list I had written of all the things that will hinder me from learning, I slumped back in my chair.

"Well, here it is God," I proclaimed.

"I haven't read a book in ten years."

"I've got a short concentration span."

"I find it hard to retain information."

"I'm easily distracted."

The list went on.

"I'm not going to be able to do it without your help."

I looked back at the book. Chapter one finished.

Tick.

Eight to go.

'Set Free to Learn' was only a small book. I ran my fingers across the words and swallowed as many practical learning tips as I could. I was hungry for any insight I could find.

The world seemed to stop. I was oblivious to anything happening around me. The only sounds were the words coming from the pages.

I took what seemed to be my first breath. I looked at my watch. I looked again. *It can't be.* I took the watch off and drew it towards my face to ensure I was seeing correctly.

I can't believe it. It's been four hours. It's a miracle.

***

The energy during orientation week was high. Every day started with praise and worship and a word of encouragement from one of the lecturers. It was so uplifting; it was like being at church every day.

Over the week we met the lecturers and received overviews of what we'd be studying in the first term.

"I'm looking forward to this subject," I said to my newfound friend, Julie, as we headed into the classroom. "The New Testament is a little easier to understand than the Old Testament."

She looked back and gave me a smile. "Let's sit over here," she said, as she pushed a couple of chairs in to get through.

The room was lined with desks joined together to make five rows. I followed her to the end desk at the back.

Glancing around the room, I studied everyone's dress, wondering how they had come to be at college.

I noticed one of the girls in front of me was wearing black stilettos. *I wonder how long she's going to survive in those? I wouldn't even make it up the stairs in them.*

My mind thought about the fly on the wall. I let out a little chuckle.

I'm here Jerry! If only you could see me now.

The class began jumping to their feet. "What's happening?" I asked Julie as I stood up. "What have I missed?"

"We're just about to do a quick quiz," she whispered. "If you answer correctly you can stay standing. If incorrect you have to sit down."

I nodded as my attention turned to the front. *I need to focus. I'd better sit at the front next time.*

***

My first assignment didn't come easily. I had moved to a little self-contained unit rented out by a family living upstairs to be closer to college. I was propped up in bed in the small room that was once part of their garage. My bed lamp was shining on the page.

'Pilgrim's Progress' was a Christian allegory written in 1678 by John Bunyan. It was known to be the most significant work of religious theological fiction in English literature. Translated into 200 languages, it had never been out of print.

The book was riveting. I felt the emotion of every trial, temptation and obstacle that Christian, the main character, faced.

I was still reading the book the night before the assignment was due. Christian met people on the path who helped him, who deceived him, people full of good will and others who made his journey hard. It was all too real. I finally closed the book and my eyes were quick to follow.

The following day I sat looking at the blank white page staring back at me. My fingers tap danced on the desk waiting for an idea. I rolled the pen back and forth. I read the book review requirements and rewrote them trying to gain a clear understanding of what was required.

The canvas in my head was empty. I didn't know where to start. My legs were moving back and forth under the desk. The roar of the lawn mower engine next door was screaming in my head.

Maybe a cup of tea will help. Thoughts of Shaz were on my mind as I walked back and forth waiting for the kettle to boil. *I wonder how she's going. I need to pop in and see her this afternoon.*

A couple of marks on the small cupboard underneath the sink caught my attention. With the spray bottle in my hand I looked around the room.

What else needs cleaning? I haven't done the shower for a while. My sheets and doona would benefit from a wash. I could wash my car.

My stomach started to rumble as I sat back down at the desk. I picked up my notebook, pen and list of requirements and locked the door behind me.

I'll be able to think more clearly down at the waterfront. I'll get something to eat while I'm out.

The pelicans were gracefully bobbing up and down with the wind stirring the water. Sailing boats were flapping in the breeze as they drifted along in the distance. I looked back at the requirements.

A few points came to mind as I sat listening to the water lapping on the stone wall. I put pen to paper quickly before they flew away. I gazed at the horizon as inspiration started to flow. My thoughts were now moving quicker than I could write.

I picked up my watch from the table. *I'm going to need an extension. At least I've started.*

Nervously submitting the book review the following day, I breathed a sigh of relief. *Better late than never.*

"That was hard," I said to Julie as we walked down the hill to the auditorium. "I loved the book but I didn't have a clue how to do a review."

She sniggered. "You've got a long way to go. Are you going to do the two years?"

I gasped. "Let me get through today first," I replied.

Learning to read and write an assignment wasn't the only new challenge in front of me.

Chapter 12 | Four Hours

***

A number of unfamiliar faces greeted me as I walked into the large shed for the information morning.

My eyes discreetly scanned the room as the children's pastor went through some of the Sunday School material. I quickly dropped my head if someone caught my eye.

"This is Mrs Blake," Pastor Mark said. "You're welcome to sit in her class tomorrow if you want to see how it works."

"I've never worked with children." I said as I gave her a tentative smile. "I've never had anything to do with children."

"You'll love them," she responded as her hand touched my arm. "They're really sweet."

The following morning I arrived early. I scanned the church auditorium looking for Mrs Blake as the worship leaders started the welcome songs. My eyes twitched. *What if she doesn't turn up? What if she's sick?*

The leaders accompanied the children to the shed. I kept to the back hoping that Mrs Blake would appear.

Children were clapping and jumping as the music started. Their faces were beaming. The young people at the front were animated. A few older boys stood to the side like fish out of water.

I relaxed as Mrs Blake popped her head around the corner. "I didn't think you were going to show," I whispered.

"Sorry," she chuckled. "I was running late so I came straight here."

I followed her around the corner to the little room.

Fourteen little eyes were looking back at me as I was introduced.

"This is Miss Nyree," Mrs Blake said. "Miss Nyree is going to join us today."

"Hi everyone," I said as I gave a wave.

"Good morning, Miss Nyree," they all replied in unison.

My heart was warmed. *How sweet.*

I sat quietly at the back as Mrs Blake read the story and placed pictures on the board beside her.

The children were mesmerised as she placed the animals two by two into the ark.

"What about dogs?" one of the little boys asked. "Did God create dogs?"

"Yes," Mrs Blake answered. "He created all the animals."

I noticed a little fluffy head popping out of one of the boy's bags.

"Is that your little friend?" I asked as we headed outside for morning tea.

He nodded.

"He's very cute," I continued. "What's his name?"

His eyes were wide as he looked up at me. "His name's Henry," he replied.

"Hi Henry," I said as I patted him on the head. "How are you today?"

"He can't talk," the little one responded. "He's a bear."

"Oh," I replied. "Sorry Henry." I turned to the little one. "Lucky he's got you to help him."

The little boy's smile went from ear to ear.

As I helped Mrs Blake tidy up, I pulled a giraffe from the felt board and placed it back on, intrigued by how it stuck.

Mrs Blake smiled. "Would you like to tell the story next week?" she asked.

My swallow was audible. "I'll think about it," I responded. "I'll get back to you."

All afternoon I thought about the children, their smiles, their attentive eyes. *Mrs Blake must be seventy. If she can do it, I'm sure I can.*

The following week I was sitting in her chair. Six months later my heart was tugged to take on a bigger challenge.

CHAPTER 13

"He's the most unlikely looking person to be working with children," I whispered to my friend. "He looks like he needs a good feed. How would he ever keep up with them?"

The Bible college auditorium was full of colour. Red, yellow, green, and orange flags were scattered across the stage. Large poster boards were painted with words to songs. A table filled with wooden crafts stood at the front next to an easel with a large flannel board.

"Geoff Yarrow is the founder of the Kids' Club Movement," the Dean said.

You could have heard a pin drop the minute Geoff opened his mouth. He spoke in the same quiet monotone voice, but everyone was captivated.

"Robert Raikes started the first Sunday School in London in 1780," he said. "Twenty years after he died one third of the population were attending Sunday Schools in England."

"In 1898, three Sunday Schools in Redfern, Sydney had four thousand children attending weekly," he continued.

My mind boggled. *That's a lot of children. It's more than a thousand in each. How would they accommodate them?*

His last statement hit me like a ball being tossed by an opponent.

"In 1953, thirty five percent of children attended Sunday school. Over thirty years this has declined to two and a half percent."

I sat staring at his board. The line had moved from across the board to a small speck on the left. *Why has attendance dropped so significantly in thirty years?*

The atmosphere changed as we all jumped to our feet. We were about to experience how a kids' club worked.

My heart responded. I took some information back to Pastor Mark hoping we could run one at our church.

"Would you consider running a kids' club?" I asked, as he tidied up after the morning's service. I put the folder on a chair to wind up the lead from the overhead projector.

"We had a guest speaker this week at college, Geoff Yarrow," I continued. My speech started to quicken with excitement. "He's developed a program for children that includes games, singing, story-time, dinner, and craft. It sounds fantastic."

Pastor Mark continued stacking the chairs.

"Geoff provides training for the leaders, promotes the Kids' Club in the local primary schools and will run the first night," I continued. "Most clubs run with thirty to forty children per week."

The numbers seemed to catch his attention. He walked over and signalled with his hand for the folder. He stood quietly scanning the pages.

"You could run it," he said as he handed the folder back.

My body was stuck, but my mind was bolting.

Me?

What?

No, no, no, no, no!

I wasn't asking if I could run it. I was hoping you would.

Exhaling, I said, "I'll think about it." Giving him a fleeting smile, I left with the folder in hand. Over the following week I studied the material and put my feelers out to gauge if anyone was interested in helping.

Chapter 13 | The Song

"It's a well-planned program with good resources," the senior pastor said. "It would be a good training ground for our young people."

After a lot of deliberation, I took the step. Our leaders did the full day training and we were at the school to promote the first night.

The children were buzzing as they picked up the aeroplanes, jewellery boxes, boats and other creations made out of paddle pop sticks and wooden blocks.

"I'm coming," a little boy said excitedly as he took a flyer. "I'm going to ask Mum as soon as I get home."

The phone rang just as I had finished checking everything was in place for the afternoon.

"I'm not able to make it tonight," my song leader said. "Something has come up."

I froze. *What am I going to do? I don't have time to find a replacement. I can't sing, but I'll have to.*

My thoughts taunted me as I remembered the day I had auditioned for the primary school choir. We only had to sing three words and include our name.

"My name is Nyree," I had sung with the sweetest voice I could muster.

The following day they announced those who were successful. I had butterflies. I didn't take my eyes off the music teacher as she called each name. I waited patiently, while desperately wanting to hear mine. Smiles were glowing on the other children's faces.

The clip board went back to her lap. I looked around the room. My heart sank. There were only two children who didn't make the choir and one of them was me.

I tried to dismiss my fear. *Geoff Yarrow did it with a room filled with a hundred children at the conference. He didn't have music or musicians. It can't be that hard.*

Cars were filing into the carpark as families lined up to sign in their children. The children's heads didn't turn back as they headed straight towards the ball game on the field.

Shrieks of excitement sounded as the children ran through the middle of the other two teams hoping to escape being eliminated.

As the game ended, they lined up like soldiers behind the coloured flags matching their name tags. They marched into the hall and took a seat.

"Hi everyone," I said as the leaders lined up beside me. "Welcome to our first night of Kids' Club."

After introducing the leaders, I picked up the first song board and encouraged everyone to jump to their feet.

The board shook to the beat of my nerves. I tried to build some momentum. I started the song.

Nobody seemed to follow.

My nerves got the better of me as my mind stammered. *I can't sing.*

I put the board down mid song and introduced the young people who were doing the memory verse. *I'll have to find someone else who can sing, for next week.*

My calm returned as I picked up the story. I had practised it multiple times the night before as Shaz sat silently as my audience.

The room was quiet. The children and leaders were transfixed as I turned each page. The tone of my voice undulated as the suspense built. I paused, leaving silence to engulf the listener. There was a complete hush as we got to the end of the story and finished with a little prayer.

It didn't take long for the noise to crescendo. The children were clambering with excitement as they lined up for their plate of chicken nuggets and chips.

"It's loud," I said to one of the leaders, "but it's beautiful. Look at the children's faces."

My head continued to spin as the children clamoured for help with the craft. Glue was going everywhere. As I glanced around, I noticed leaders at the other tables looking frazzled. I penned a note in my mind to order extra craft and do a practice run before the following week.

The momentum grew. Children started taking their crafts to school for show and tell. Others invited friends. By the end of the year we had forty children attending each week.

Chapter 13 | The Song

Everything was rolling. It seemed natural to return to Bible College the following year to complete my Diploma of Ministry.

***

Three days before I was due to return, I was sitting on the back deck. The trees were swaying in the breeze as the sun started to set. An image flashed through my mind; I was sitting in a large harvester that was travelling around and around a square paddock. I shook my head as I shifted my gaze back to the trees. It was still there. It made me nervous but I was peaceful.

I rang Jan. "Something strange has happened," I said as I described the picture. "I can't seem to budge it. It doesn't make sense."

"Have you considered God might be trying to speak to you?" she asked. "Is He calling you to do something?"

Standing motionless, I tried to calculate her question. "I, I don't know," I responded. "I didn't know He did that."

"Why don't you pray and ask Him" she said. "I'll pray, too. I'll call you in a couple of days to follow up."

There was no light bulb moment, but deep down I sensed I shouldn't be heading back to Bible College. My thoughts were in overdrive.

I've got the diploma to complete. I've got children's church, religious education, Kids' Club and the volunteers who visit Shaz and the residents at Daisy Lodge. I've only got three days before college starts back. I'll have to repay the Austudy I received over the holidays.

Peace hung over me like a canopy quieting my mind and quelling my resistance. I knew it was the right decision, so I headed into the Bible College to give them the news.

"Nyree isn't coming back," the lecturer said as the dean stood in her doorway.

"Why not?" He asked as he glanced in my direction.

I sat silently for a moment. *How am I going to explain what I saw? Is he going to think I'm nuts? Will he try and dissuade me?*

"I'm going to go and work with children," I replied.

"Where?" the dean asked.

My eyes darted as I tried to create a plan on the spot. Nothing was forthcoming.

Shrugging my shoulders, I replied, "I'm not too sure. I'm just not coming back."

"That's okay," he replied. "Second year is for leaders anyway."

His words pierced my stomach. I felt undermined, disempowered, and insignificant. I was gutted. *Who does he think he is?* I smiled dismissing the comment, but I couldn't budge it from my mind.

He was a man I respected and held in high regard. He invested so much in me throughout the year, only to withdraw his encouragement with a few words.

I was hurt and so angry. I grappled with his comment as I fought back. *He's not God anyway. What would he know?*

On the way home I dropped into the Kids' Club Resource Centre to collect some craft packs to start the year.

The dusty air caught my breath as I entered the shed. Craft stacked in boxes from floor to ceiling lined the walls. Choosing packs was like choosing my favourite lollies at the shop.

Excitedly picking a number of craft packs, I placed them on the floor, slowly eliminating a few, finishing with the four I needed.

"Would you like help packing your shelves?" I asked Wilma as I placed the craft packs on the counter. "I'm not going back to Bible College, so I have some time on my hands."

Wilma looked back at me like I had handed her a thousand dollars. "That would be great," she replied. "We'd never say no to extra help."

As I turned to leave, a number of elderly men walked into the warehouse. Their smiles popping out from behind faces covered in dust.

"It looks like its cuppa time," Wilma said. "Would you like to join us?"

The smell of home baked banana cake teased my senses as she lifted the lid from the container.

"I won't say no," I replied.

One by one the men picked up a piece of cake and introduced themselves, sharing how they became involved with the Kids' Club ministry. Some of them had volunteered their time for years cutting timber and wooden blocks for the craft models.

***

One afternoon I was putting pom-poms into the craft packs when Geoff Yarrow arrived. I had never met anyone so passionate in sharing the Gospel with children. He rattled off statistics like they were placed on a screen in front of him.

"Why don't you go out on the road with him?" Wilma asked "I'm sure he'd appreciate the help."

"I'd love to," I responded.

I followed Geoff to church presentations, training sessions, lunchtime school promotions and the first Kids' Club nights at a number of churches. I gleaned everything I could from his stories, his passion, and ten years of experience.

"Why don't I help you do up some training boards?" Geoff asked as we returned from the last club. "You could manage Queensland?"

I was caught off guard. My eyes bugged out as I stood silently.

Queensland?

I was in a whirlwind. My head was nodding before I had time to count the cost.

It's voluntary. How will I be able to pay my bills?

Photos

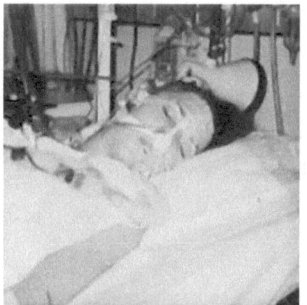

Intensive Care

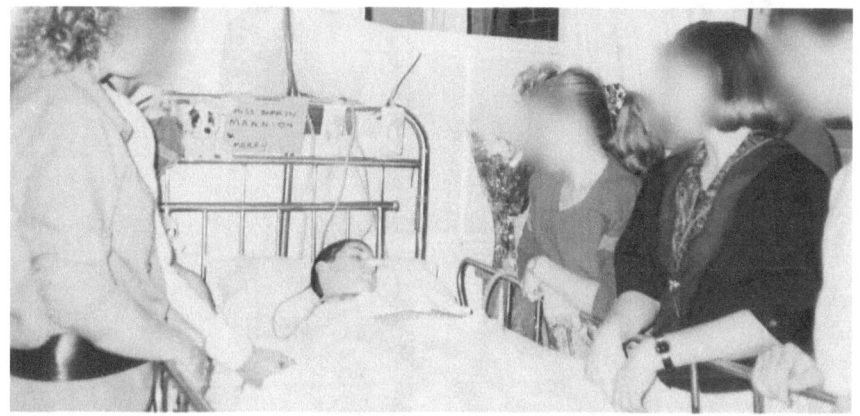

Sharyn's 24th Birthday

Time Outside

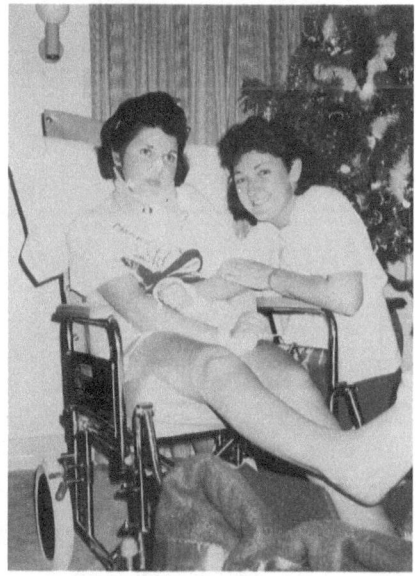

Coming Home

Head Injury Awareness Week
Brisbane City Mall

Hydrotherapy

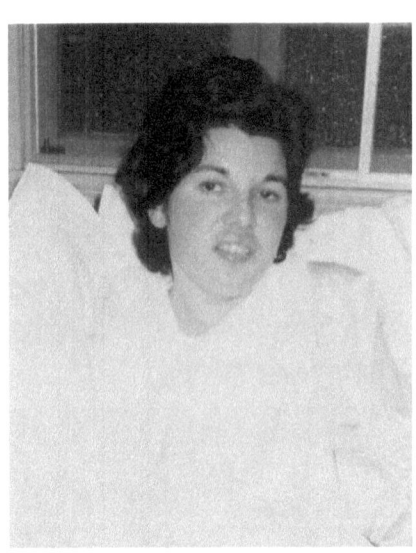
A Good Day

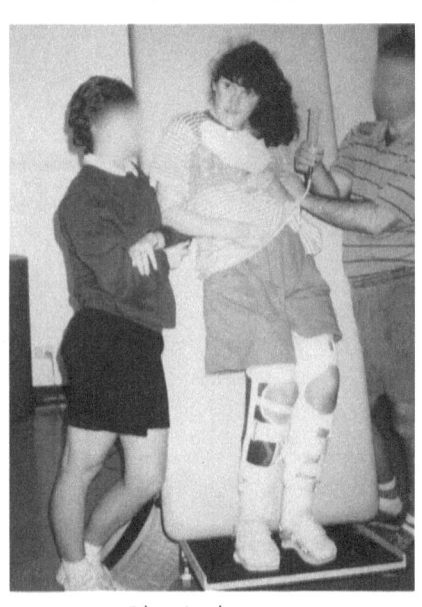
Physiotherapy

Hayman Island Familiarisation

Bird Man Jump

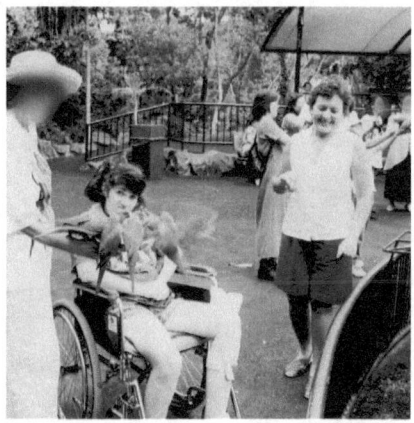

Currumbin Bird Sanctuary
Spelling on an Alphabet Board

Kids' Club

Happy Birthday

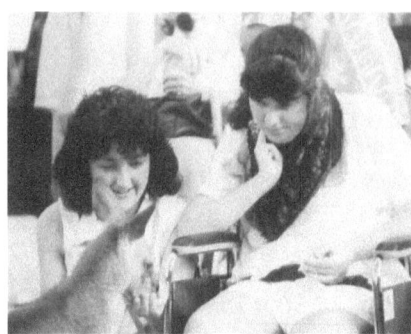
At the Zoo

Bachelor of Ministry

Deer Sanctuary

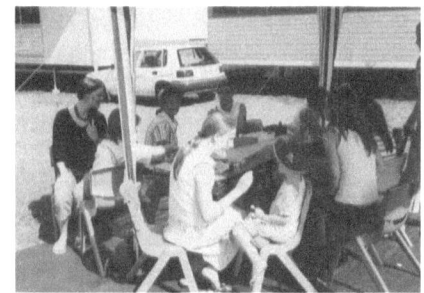
Face Painting

Solomon Islands

School Chaplaincy

Chaplaincy Camp

Chaplaincy Camp

Modified Vehicle Handover

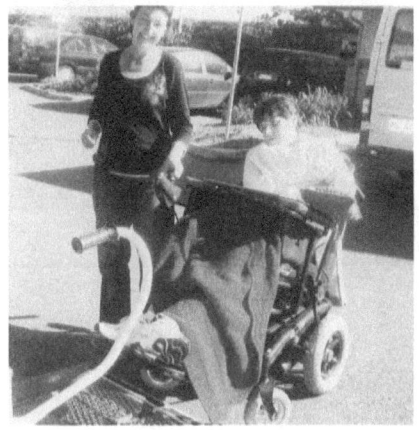
Out and About

Turning the Sod

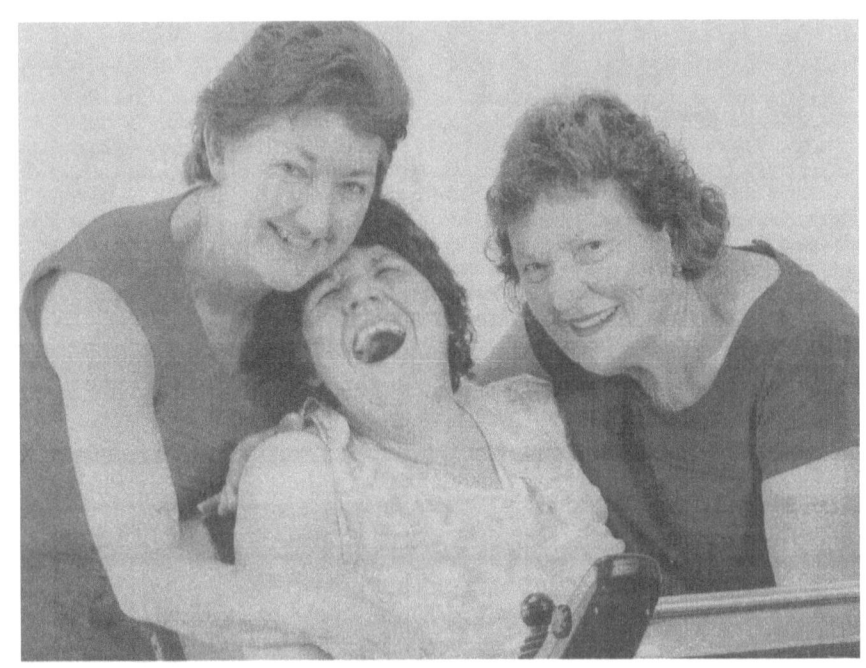
Newspaper Clipping- Celebrating a Home for Life

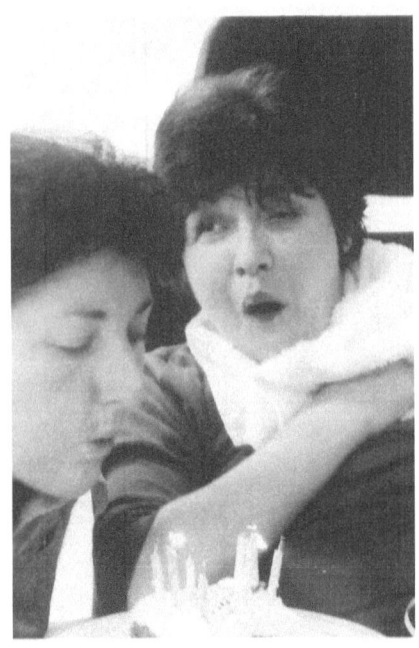
My Birthday

Sharyn Pre-Accident

CHAPTER 14
Red Sea Moment

I stood staring at the training boards, manuals, and the map of Queensland.

"Just tell my stories until you get your own," Geoff said as he hopped in the car to return to Sydney.

During my first presentation I was sitting in the front pew next to the minister's wife. After being introduced as the guest speaker the reverend said, "Let's pray."

Closing my eyes as I was accustomed to in the church I regularly attended, my ears pricked as I heard everyone praying in unison. I glanced up and noticed the minister's wife holding a book.

She gently moved one towards me. I nodded, smiled and opened it to wherever the page landed. I moved my mouth. There was no point trying to work out the prayer they were reading.

My nerves disappeared as I passionately shared some of Geoff's stories about the formation of the Kids' Club program.

"Over the past ten years the organisation has started three hundred and fifty clubs in NSW alone," I said. "Hundreds of others have been established in other states of Australia."

"Parents love them," I continued as enthusiastic faces looked back at me. "It gives them time to get some late-night shopping done while their children are meeting their friends, having a meal, and hearing the Gospel. The children love the craft and can't wait to get back the next week for more."

Throughout the following year I established clubs in different denominations. Their forms and methods of worship were quite varied, but the excitement and enthusiasm of the children was always the same.

I was living simply but the constant worry about where my next dollar was coming from wore me out.

"I'm going to give it up," I said to Mum as I sneezed into my arm, trying to avoid Shaz who was sitting beside me. "It's a wonderful ministry, but I need to pay the bills."

"You can live in the cottage for six months while I renovate it," she replied. "It might help a little."

"It'd be a great help," I replied. "It's not a long-term solution, though. I can't keep living like this. I'm nursing a cold every other week. I need to go back to paid work."

The following day a comment was made that astounded me.

We were gathering with leaders from the newly established Kids' Clubs for a BBQ. Picnic rugs were splayed everywhere. The smell of sausages and onions beckoned me.

"One of the children's parents told me her son is more confident since he's been coming to the Kids' Club," Julianne said as a few of us stood swapping stories. "She said he struggles socially but he's been making new friends."

Fiona responded. "One of mine told me her daughter has increased helping around the house. She said her manners have improved and she's getting on better with her sister. The parents love it," she continued. "For some they use it as a reward at the end of the week."

The feedback was encouraging but I was perplexed. I hadn't let on that I was leaving, but I couldn't see an alternative. Towards the end of the afternoon we gathered into small groups to pray for one another.

"Geoff told me he has helped many like you to get started with the ministry," one of the ladies said. "You're the only one who's stayed committed to these kids."

Chapter 14 | Red Sea Moment

As I stood motionless, my thoughts raced. *If only she knew what I'm about to do.*

The following morning, I headed to the resource centre to tell them I was leaving. Leila the manager was sitting at her desk.

"I've got some good news for you," she said as I placed my bag under the counter.

"We had a discussion after the picnic yesterday," she continued. "We've decided to pay you two days per week."

My head dropped into my hands as the tension unravelled in my shoulders. *My goodness, how did they know?*

"We're also going to charge the churches for the training sessions," she continued.

Tears rolled down my face as I peeled back my hands.

"I was just about to resign," I blurted.

Nobody blinked. Everyone was silent.

"I can't believe it," I said as I scratched my head.

Leila was shaking hers. "Me neither," she replied. "The timing's perfect."

The atmosphere lightened as we all realised what had just unfolded.

***

It wasn't long before another miracle occurred.

Peter, a local evangelist, bounded into the resource centre. His enthusiasm was tangible.

"We've got a bunch of young people coming from America," he said, "to run programs in the high schools. We'd like to host a children's program at the waterfront while they are here."

My heart skipped excitedly as he shared his ideas.

"You might want to get those folders out," Wilma said as her eyes caught mine.

Peter looked at us both inquisitively.

"I put this together a year ago," I said as I handed him a folder. "It's been sitting in the filing cabinet ever since."

His eyes widened. "This is amazing," he replied. "Would you be happy to share this at the Minister's Fraternal next week?"

My stomach was churning. *Who am I to speak to ministers? I'm young. I'm a female.*

The desire to be involved was the only thing that got me to the meeting. I nervously greeted a number of the ministers on arrival and sat towards the back.

As Peter gave an overview, I scanned my list. *The groundwork is already done. Everything's in place. I'll just need to be there on the day.*

My mouth was dry as I walked to the front. I distributed the folders, hoping there would be fewer eyes looking at me when I spoke.

"I had an idea a year ago," I said as I lifted up the folders. "I spent days developing an outline of how to run an outreach and what would be required from Geoff Yarrow's material. It ended up being filed away as no one was keen to get behind it."

"It's all here," I continued. "We'd love to be involved."

***

A few months later, Peter called me inviting me to travel with a team of young people to the Solomon Islands to run a Children's Discipleship Training Program with the local church leaders. I was given the job of overseeing the girls as a bonus.

You could almost smell the stifling heat as we arrived in Honiara. Sweat was running down my back as we walked past the towering palm trees towards our transport.

"Who wants to ride in the front?" Peter called.

Everyone's hands disappeared as the lure of travelling in the back of an open truck was before us.

The hot wind pushed against us as we bumped along waving to locals strolling down the road.

A number of Solomon Islanders had gathered to greet us as we arrived at the transit centre.

Chapter 14 | Red Sea Moment

Chairs were scattered along the four walls of the living area. Platters of sandwiches and fruit lined the tables. The large windows made way for the hot breeze to flow.

"Just relax," Peter said as we sat around getting to know each other. "We'll have prayer and a planning meeting this afternoon."

Relaxing didn't come easy for me. Time was precious back home. I was always trying to squeeze something else in; work, study, Shaz, church.

My mind was in overdrive. *Shouldn't we be planning for tomorrow? Do we need to do something for dinner? Who's picking us up to take us to the field?*

I walked around the house and picked a beautiful hibiscus from the garden to place on the table. Most of the girls were lying on their beds, overcome by the change in the temperature. There wasn't much we could do but wait. I read for a while trying to slow my mind.

The following day we boarded a ship to Auki. The temperature dial had been turned up even further. Locals were carrying washers to regularly wipe their brow. People were scattered throughout the boat inside and out as chatter and singing filled the air.

After settling into the house that would be our home for the week, we walked up the dirt road to the church.

"I hope they're still here when we finish," I said to one of the girls on our team as I placed my shoes in the line at the front door. "I can't stand not having something on my feet."

The Solomon Islanders left their voices with their shoes as they sat quietly preparing their hearts for worship. The women sat on the left whilst the men sat on the right.

"Shh," I whispered as I heard our young people talking, unaware of the silence surrounding them.

Leaders wearing colourful shirts complimenting their contagious smiles stepped forward to sing. Joy flooded the church as their melodious voices filled the air.

I didn't know whether to sing or just bask in the atmosphere. I did both. I listened, I sang, I prayed.

The Solomon Islander's grace and beauty overwhelmed me.

Kneeling down, I took off my watch and placed it on the stool in front of me. I was completely unencumbered. I felt so humble, so free, until something tugged my heart.

Looking up at the lady in front of me I started to pray.

After the session, I tapped her on the shoulder and greeted her with a smile. "This might seem strange," I said, "but I feel prompted to give you my watch."

Tears burst forth from her eyes and streamed down her face as she stood holding my hand. I sat down beside her. The silence seemed natural.

"Adam, the pastor, is my husband," she said quietly. "He left his teaching job years ago to serve God. I fully supported him, but it hasn't always been easy. Sometimes we don't even know where our next meal is coming from."

She took a deep breath. "God is reminding me He's always with us. He'll always provide."

"I know," I replied. "I've seen it with my own eyes."

We sat for a while exchanging stories before praying for each other and our families.

The night was as hot as the day. I could hear voices outside and something scratching under the house. Melinda, one of the girls on the team, was restless. Every time she moved, I stirred.

"Are you okay?" I asked when dawn broke. "You were tossing and turning all night."

She shook her head. "I had a nightmare," she replied as she sat down on the bed. "I dreamt God asked me to speak in the marketplace and I was too scared. I struggled and struggled. I couldn't do it."

I bit my lip. "I'm glad it was you and not me," I replied. "I wouldn't have the courage either. Would you like me to pray for you? I'm sure God understands."

As we prepared for the last day of training, the Bible story of the lame man being healed hovered in my mind. It pulled on my heart strings as I thought of Shaz. Sadness overwhelmed me. *I've prayed for her many times. Why hasn't God healed her? I know He can.*

Movement caught my attention. My jaw dropped as Peter advised we were going to run a program at the marketplace that afternoon. I scanned

Chapter 14 | Red Sea Moment

the place looking for Melinda as my thoughts darted straight back to her nightmare.

As we arrived at the markets, the story of the lame man was still hovering in my thoughts. People sat waving their branches, brushing the flies from the fish and vegetables lined up for sale.

My body shook as the team started to sing. My heart was pounding.

"Peter, I think God wants me to share a message with these people," I said. "The story of the lame man has been in my mind all day."

His smile broadened. "We'll sing a couple more songs," he replied. "Then I'll introduce you."

My nerves escalated. *Is anyone going to hear me? I'm going to have to talk really loudly. Will they even understand me?*

I started to recite the story from Acts chapter 3. "Peter and John were heading to the temple to pray," I said. "A man crippled from birth asked them for money. They gave him much more than that."

Opening the Bible in my hand I read.

> Peter said, 'silver or gold I do not have, but what I have I give you. In the name of Jesus Christ of Nazareth, walk.' Taking him by the right hand, he helped him up, and instantly the man's feet and ankles became strong. He jumped to his feet and began to walk. Then he went with them into the temple courts, walking and jumping and praising God.

Walking towards one of the ladies selling fish, I said, "Maybe you are looking for something today. You're hoping that people will buy your fish. God has so much more for you. He wants to encourage you. He wants to lift you up. Just reach out to him in prayer. He will meet you there."

I stopped as my words dried up.

Peter stepped forward and invited people to respond if they wanted someone from the team to pray with them.

Standing amazed that I had found such boldness and courage to share what God had put in my heart, my mind turned towards home. My heart was full of hope of what God could do for Shaz. I couldn't wait to get back to pray for her.

CHAPTER 15
Fire Works

Shaz was just the same, when I arrived home. There was no expression that she'd missed me or was excited to see me. She was settled most of the time unless she had pain, which was evident when she extended her legs, her muscles contracted in her arms or her facial muscles tightened.

Deep down I was hoping there would be a greater response after not seeing me for two weeks. I sat sharing my stories with her about the people and their culture, the watch and the market place before saying another prayer. I placed my hand on her shoulder and boldly asked God to heal her.

When no miracle was forthcoming, I convinced myself that it would happen in God's time. *I know He can and I know He will, when He's ready.*

***

Later that year Edwin, a church leader from the Solomon Islands and a group of young people came to Australia. They had two nights staying with Peter and his wife Angela before heading to a prayer base in Stanthorpe. It was winter so our first point of call was the op shop.

"Pick whatever you need," I said to Edwin as I handed him a large bag. "Make sure everyone gets a couple of jumpers and long pants. It's going to get colder."

I dropped into Peter and Angela's house the following morning to see the team.

"How was your first night in Brisbane?" I asked as they sat around the dining table filled with toast, cereal and juice.

Edwin looked like he had just walked out of an industrial freezer. "It's cold," he said as he rubbed his arms.

My smile broadened. *Wait till we get to Stanthorpe.*

Having driven Sharyn's van for a number of years, I was designated as one of the drivers for the twelve-seater bus. The two-and-a-half-hour journey south was filled with singing, chatter and the occasional strange smell.

The prayer base was stationed on a farming property surrounded by bushland and clear blue sky. Condensation created clouds in the air as everyone hopped off the bus.

"I'm smoking," one of the young boys said as he puffed air from his lips.

"Me too," said another as he moved his mouth in different directions.

After lunch we strolled around the property, readjusting our ears to the tranquillity and our pace to that of being freed from the hustle and bustle of the city. I chuckled as I remembered my struggle to relax on my first afternoon in the Solomon Islands.

Young people from the local youth groups gathered in the converted shed for praise and worship that evening.

The atmosphere changed the minute the Solomon Islander young people started to sing. My heart moved as I joined in with the chorus.

Their songs washed over me like refreshing rain pouring down from the clouds.

"They're so beautiful," I whispered to one of the girls standing beside me. "They have such a unique gift."

After a number of songs, Matt the farm owner was invited to share his story.

I could hear his heartache as he shared their journey through the drought over the past two years.

Chapter 15 | Fire Works

"We lost the first crop," he said, "but we ploughed the ground and planted again. At times, clouds hovered in the sky raising our hope only to fly away without a drop. We lost the second and the third crop."

My heart sank as his voice quivered.

"Our workers grew increasingly discouraged," he continued, "but we couldn't give up. We knew if the rains came and there was no seed planted, we'd have no harvest."

A hush fell over the room as he paused. He looked around at the young people.

"Our situation is similar to faith," he continued. "You may have been praying and sharing God's word with others who are hard, disinterested and even antagonistic towards God. You may have been doing it for years without seeing any change or response."

A number of family members and friends flashed through my mind as his words resonated in my heart.

"It's discouraging," he continued "but you can't give up. You have to trust God and believe He is at work in their lives. In your life."

As he finished speaking, we were invited to gather into small groups to pray for the farmers, their families and the much-needed rain.

Later that evening as I lay listening to the trees brushing against the house, I thought about the faith, resilience and determination Matt and the other farmers had shown through their years of hardship. *Hope is their key to survival, just like our family.*

I hadn't been asleep long when I was woken by the same sound I had heard in the Solomon Islands so many times. It was 3:00am and the Solomon Islanders were up and worshipping God.

I can't stay in bed. I don't want to miss out. I want to be with them, I want to worship God with the same enthusiasm and joy.

As I walked towards the shed, the cold frost bit my nose. I chuckled as I saw Edwin almost sitting on top of the heater with the other young people sitting on top of him.

Their eyes greeted me as I joined their warm huddle.

***

The Solomon Islanders' commitment and zealousness for God was just as strong as we gathered with the young people from churches all around Brisbane for the three-day camp a couple of days later.

After a morning of Bible teaching and interaction in small groups we headed to the beach for the afternoon.

"Can you hold onto these?" one of the young girls asked as she handed me a watch, a ring and a lighter. "I'm going for a swim."

I placed them in my pocket and didn't think anything more about them until the evening when we were back in the hall, preparing music, drama, and messages for the church services for the following day.

During the time of praise and worship, my hand started to shake as it brushed past my pocket. I tried to steady it with my other hand, but the intensity grew. I pulled out the watch, lighter, and ring.

Walking to the front, I spoke to Peter, "I think God wants to speak through these items," I said as I placed them on the table beside him. The shaking stopped the moment I let go of them, but my heart was still racing.

Peter motioned to the band to quieten the music.

"I believe God wants to speak to us about our time, our relationships and addictions," he said as he held up the items. "There are many things in the world that can draw our attention and affection away from God."

"Are you wasting time each day on computer games, TV, caught up in pornography or drugs, unable to break free? Are you in a relationship you know is not good for you?"

"God has a plan and a purpose for your life. He's calling you. He wants to empower you. He wants to provide for you. He wants to heal you, deliver you and set you free. If God is speaking to you," Peter continued. "If you know something isn't right... If you want to put it right with God, I want you to come to the front."

I stepped back to let a young guy past. He was shaking; his lips were quivering as tears ran down his face. He was moving towards the front. I could hear the shuffle of others following.

A number of our leaders gathered around them to pray. Some lingered at the front for a time.

Chapter 15 | Fire Works

We moved into small groups where the young people shared what had just transpired. Their sharing turned into a message for the church services the following morning. 'Sacrifice and Surrender' became the theme.

The young people were nervous though they stepped out of their comfort zones the following morning to lead worship, share their stories and a message from God. Change was happening before our eyes. Their fears turned to boldness. Confidence beamed from their faces as they took on the challenge.

***

The following week the Solomon Islanders and young people from the camp gathered again in a local park.

"We need to call the young people of our nation back to God," Peter said as we stood standing around a map of Australia. "We've got eighteen months before we enter the new millennium."

Peter invited us to sign our name on the map if we were willing to surrender our lives and commit to prayer. One by one the young people picked up a marker pen, knelt down, and signed their name.

A rustling in the trees caught our attention. We could hear voices in the distance. I stood upright scouring the area like a lifeguard. My body tensed as goosebumps tingled my skin. The lighting was dim making it hard to see what was going on beyond the trees.

A few minutes later, Melinda, one of the youth leaders, was running towards us with two boys hot on her heels.

"What's going on?" Peter asked in a serious tone. "Is everything okay?"

"Julius and Jonathan travelled down with me tonight," Melinda replied with excitement. "They've been challenged by what's happening here. They've just run and binned their marijuana. They want to turn their lives around."

We all cheered with excitement as they knelt and added their names to the map.

It was the birth of a youth prayer movement in Australia. Peter had been commissioned as the Youth Ambassador to the South Pacific and the fire was spreading.

***

On the last Friday of every month we gathered to pray. Young people gave up their usual entertainment and social outings to seek God on behalf of our leaders, our communities, and our nation.

As the countdown to the new millennium got closer, the media hype escalated.

"The Y2K Millennium Bug will cause computers around the world to fall at the stroke of midnight," the news reporter said. "The year 2000 is indistinguishable from 1900 due to many programs representing four-digit years, with only the final two digits."

Fear that planes would fall from the sky, power systems would fail, bank accounts would be wiped out, and nuclear missiles would inadvertently launch, were fuelling the media.

The fears were far from our minds as we gathered in the exhibition grounds to pray on the last night of the century.

Five hundred young people full of hope and enthusiasm for what lay ahead was like fire raging through a forest that couldn't be extinguished. The energy was electric.

Youth leaders were rotating in teams to lead praise and worship, prayers of repentance, messages of hope, testimonies and a commitment to follow God.

"Please have mercy on us, oh God," I cried as we gathered into small groups to pray. "Have mercy on our community, our city, our nation."

"Raise up Godly leaders to govern our land," I continued. "Give them your wisdom and courage to make Godly decisions. Please guide them as they serve our country, our people."

It was 11:55pm. A fleeting thought passed through my mind. *What if this is it? What if the world does end? Am I ready to meet Jesus face to face?*

My thoughts were arrested as the countdown began.

10

9

8

"Well here I am God," I prayed. "Please forgive me and have mercy on me."

7

6

5

"Have mercy on my family."

4

3

2

"Have mercy on Shaz."

1!

The field erupted. Shouts of joy went off like firecrackers as the fireworks filled the sky. In all the excitement no one stopped to realise the world hadn't ended. It had just begun.

CHAPTER 16
Chocolate

My eyes looked straight ahead as the speech therapist delivered the news. "Sharyn's results were positive," she said as she handed Mum the Video Fluoroscopy report. "Unfortunately, staff can't feed her," she continued. "There's too much risk of aspiration. Food or fluid could go into her lungs."

I took a deep breath. *Why is everything so hard? Mum is going to be devastated. She's been feeding Shaz for years.*

A few weeks earlier the speech therapist had stood motionless watching Sharyn suck on the chocolate Mum had placed under her tongue. The fear on her face turned to amazement as she realised what Sharyn could do.

Mum placed the report in the bag as she stood up. "Okay," she replied as she turned towards the door to leave.

My tongue was flapping on the roof of my mouth.

"I bet they don't want to do it because it's more work," I said to Mum as we retreated to the patio. "She saw with her own eyes; Sharyn can swallow safely. What's wrong with these people?"

"We'll keep feeding her at home," Mum replied in a quiet tone. "At least she's getting some taste and stimulation."

Thoughts tumbled around in my head for days. There's got to be a way. Being able to eat could only benefit Sharyn. She would have more interaction with others and would experience different tastes and textures.

I'm not going to give up. I'll find a way.

***

The following week I was sitting with Dad in the living room sharing a packet of his favourite barbeque chips. I had returned back to Bible College to complete a Bachelor of Ministry and was in my last year.

"I wonder if they'll let me feed Sharyn?" I said. "I could finish my course by correspondence. I'd be able to give her lunch and bring her home three days a week."

Dad gave me a serious look. "Only you can make that decision," he responded. "It's pretty big and you'll be responsible for the outcomes." He put the packet down on the table. "You need to consider Shaz too," he continued. "If you change your mind it will hurt her."

His words weighed on my shoulders like sandbags securing a marquee. The realisation that my choices had consequences and ultimately affected others stared back at me every time I looked in the mirror.

It didn't deter me. I called the dean of the college.

"Is there any way I can finish my course externally?" I asked. "I need to be home to help a family member."

He was willing to make a special case, in light of our circumstances.

***

When I dropped in to collect my course notes, I groaned as I looked at the mound of material the lecturer was carrying.

"That's a copy for both of us, isn't it?" I asked as he placed it on the counter.

He shook his head. "No. That's your copy."

"All of it?" I replied as I stood staring at the pile.

A smile crossed his face. "All of it."

Chapter 16 | Chocolate

The pile sat on my desk looking at me for two weeks. My unit had never been so clean and tidy. I cooked more than I usually did and found other things that all of a sudden became urgent.

I cleaned around the pile. I moved it to a chair. I sat on the floor working to avoid it, but my time was up.

I'm going to have to find a system. I can't leave it any longer. I've put it off long enough.

Wading through the overview, I broke each section into piles and calculated how much time I had. I added deadlines into a spreadsheet for each section to be completed.

"Can you keep a copy of this?" I asked Mum.

"What is it?" she replied.

"It's a copy of my deadlines, I need you to check that I'm reaching them. I also need you to tell me that Sharyn can't come home if I haven't got them done."

"That's a bit harsh," she responded.

"It's the only thing that will drive me and keep me on track. I don't want to let Shaz down."

***

The following day I was standing in the nurse unit manager's office.

"Can I have permission to feed Sharyn at the facility?" I asked. "Mum has been feeding her nightly. We'd like to increase it to lunchtime three times a week."

My lip curled as I waited for a response. I could hear the ceiling fan humming above. *Please say yes. Please say yes.*

"I'll okay it," she replied. "You'll need to speak to the dietician as we'll need to adjust her peg feed."

I tried to conceal my excitement.

"It will be at your own risk," she continued. "You will need to let Julie in the kitchen know the day before so she can prepare the food."

"Thank you," I said as I nodded in agreement. "I'll be careful."

My hand was shaking the first day I fed Shaz. Eyes were on us from every direction. Feeding her at home was so much easier. "Smell this, Shaz," I said as I lifted a spoonful towards her nose, "It's pureed chicken, peas, corn, and carrot."

The room was quiet. The TV was turned off to reduce noise and distraction whilst residents were eating.

I didn't breathe until she had cleared her first mouthful. My heart was racing. My mouth opened every time I turned the spoon to place food on her tongue.

The RN was beside me the minute Sharyn spluttered. The nurse's eyes were wide, her body tense.

She blinked once she realised Sharyn was okay. She continued administering the medications, though stayed close by.

Staff became a little more relaxed over the following weeks as they became more familiar with Sharyn's coughing reflex.

"Don't choke on my shift," the RN joked as she walked past. "There's too much paperwork."

After turning my head to make sure she was joking, I whispered to Shaz. "She's getting used to the idea. Hopefully we can get to a place where they'll feed you."

The months passed quickly. I managed to stay on track with my study. There was never a day that Mum had to say Sharyn couldn't come home.

***

After feeding her for a year we requested a second Video Fluoroscopy.

A new speech therapist was assigned to travel with us. I felt sorry for her as it was her first day.

I noticed a smile creeping onto Mum's face as the doctor walked towards us. "It's the same lady we saw last time," she whispered.

The doctor's expression changed as she extended a hand to greet us. "Haven't I assessed your daughter before?" she asked.

Mum nodded. "Sharyn had a Video Fluoroscopy last year."

Silence fell over the room. The speech therapist was looking at the floor. Her cheeks were getting redder.

Chapter 16 | Chocolate

"Why are you back again?" she asked as she looked at Sharyn.

"Staff at the facility where Sharyn lives wouldn't feed her due to the associated risk of aspiration," Mum replied. She looked at me. "Nyree was given permission to feed her at the facility and has done so for the last twelve months."

I gave her a fleeting smile as I put my hand on Sharyn's shoulder.

"We want to get to the place where staff will feed her," Mum continued.

The doctor's brow furrowed. Her lips were pursed and her chin was raised. She led us into the room. It wasn't as daunting this time as we knew what to expect.

Having mixed the chalky white metallic compound into Sharyn's food, I gave her the first mouthful. The radiographer moved the x-ray camera near her throat as she swallowed.

Standing still, the doctor and speech therapist watched the monitor closely. Movements of her throat and oesophagus showed on the screen as the x-ray beam passed through her body.

"Can you give Sharyn another mouthful please?" the doctor asked.

The minute the Doctor finished she turned to the speech therapist. "Sharyn can swallow safely and has good coughing reflexes," she said. "I want you to take this lady home and give her whatever she needs."

Mum's eyes were twinkling as the speech therapist nodded in agreement. "Yes," she replied. "I'll take the results back to the nurse unit manager."

"What are the odds that we'd get the same specialist?" I said to Mum as we headed to the van.

Mum glanced at me with the same look I had seen many times. It was the look of victory, with the 'how-many-times-have-we-got-to-do-this' look all in one.

Staff were gathered at the front door when we arrived back.

"How did she go?" The RN asked as we wheeled Sharyn up the path. I stood back and let the speech therapist lead.

"They've confirmed Sharyn can swallow safely," she replied. "The doctor has encouraged us to provide vitamised food for Sharyn as required."

The staff erupted with cheers and hugs. I got goosebumps.

"That's wonderful," the RN responded. "We better go and order her food now."

I was too stunned to say anything. *Why was it so hard the last time? Our persistence and hard work have finally paid off. It's been worth it.*

"We'll leave the peg in for a month," the RN said when she returned from the kitchen. "We want to make sure Sharyn has time to adjust and everything goes well before we remove it permanently."

The day Sharyn pulled the feeding tube out six months earlier flashed through my mind.

"Can you take Sharyn to emergency?" Mum had pleaded on the phone. "I'm unable to get away from work. They need to put a new peg in before the site closes up."

"I'll be there in 10 minutes, Mum." I was running. Keys, bag, towel, wipes, spare pad, notebook, pen.

As I arrived, the nurse unit manager had Shaz at the front gate.

"Do you want a staff member to go with you?" she asked as she gave me Sharyn's medical chart.

"We'll be okay," I responded. "Won't we Shaz?"

As we pulled up to the emergency department, my eyes scanned the number of people in the waiting room. My heart started to race. I went to the front counter.

"Daisy Lodge has called ahead," the receptionist said. "The doctor will be with you shortly."

Breathing a sigh of relief, my eyes darted around the room trying to find somewhere I could position Sharyn's chair without obstructing anyone. Eyes were looking at us from every direction. I felt overwhelmed.

I picked up a brochure so I could get some reprieve.

"Sharyn," the nurse called.

Wow. That was quick, thankfully.

We followed the nurse down the corridor. "I'll get a wardsman to help slide Sharyn onto the bed," she said as she pulled the blue curtain across.

I leant on the bed next to her. The little space was well equipped but impersonal. The beeping of monitors and smell of disinfectant were all too familiar.

My temperature was rising as I struggled to release the side of Sharyn's chair. "It's been a while since I've done it," I said nervously as the wardsman stood over me. "It usually drops down when you pull this lever."

He pushed the side slightly which released the pin.

Thank goodness. "Thank you," I replied.

We slid Sharyn across to the bed and elevated her head with a couple of pillows.

"The procedure will take 30-40 minutes," the doctor said as he looked at his clipboard. "A flexible tube will be passed through her mouth into her stomach to enable me to see inside."

I cringed.

"I'll place the tube through the incision in the skin and abdominal wall, where she's pulled the last one out," he continued. "A balloon and another small mushroom shaped piece of plastic will hold the tube inside the stomach."

Sitting in the long, sterile, lonesome hallway staring at the blank walls, my eyes kept looking back at the clock. I looked at my diary. I looked back at the wall.

What's that strange noise? I leant forward, tuning my ear. *It's piercing. Where's it coming from?* I looked up and down the hallway. There was no one around.

I gasped as I jumped to my feet. *It's Sharyn. She's distressed. She's never verbalised before. I couldn't swallow. My stomach twisted. What's happening in there?*

The noise stopped. I kept walking up and down the hallway. I wanted to vomit. I wanted to cry. I wanted to go in.

The door opened. I raced to her. She was sweating. Her muscles were tight. Her fists were trembling balls.

"We had to make a new incision," the doctor said. "We thought it would be safer."

I felt intimidated. I wanted to ask them if they anesthetised the site, everything within me was telling me they hadn't. I was too scared.

Sitting in recovery I held Shaz hand and stroked her arm. "I'm so sorry, Shaz," I whispered. "It must have been so painful. I shouldn't have left you on your own. I'll never, never leave you again no matter what the procedure. I promise."

A month later the peg tube was removed; it was a cause for great celebration. It was the last invasive tube Sharyn had. Our faith, belief, and determination had helped Sharyn achieve another milestone and it wasn't the only reason to celebrate.

CHAPTER 17
No to Cheese

Staff were clamouring as I walked in the front door. Their faces were shining like the sun's rays as their voices echoed in all directions.

"Happy New Year!" I said as I stood barricaded in the hallway.

"It is!" a staff member replied.

I stood wondering what was going on when a nurse blurted, "Sharyn spoke last night."

My emotions surged through my body as the staff clapped with excitement.

"We were having a party," the staff member continued. "Jim randomly asked Shaz if she would like some cheese."

Glancing at Jim, his teeth were shining whiter than his blonde hair. His blue eyes sparked as he gently nodded. "She said no," he said as his hands shook with glee.

My thoughts were turning like a spinning top as I stood looking back at him.

"No," I whispered. "I can't believe it. That's amazing." *I want to get to her. I want to hear it for myself.*

Shaz was sitting with other residents on the patio. The large trees were casting shadows sheltering them from the summer sun.

"Hi Shaz," I said as I bent down to give her a hug. "I hear you don't like cheese."

Pulling a chair up beside her I asked, "Do you like chocolate?"

Staff had encircled us like hawks.

Holding onto her chair, I waited for a response, any response.

"Shaz, would you like some chocolate?" I asked.

I asked again.

Nothing!

"That's okay," I said as I shrugged my shoulders trying to hide my disappointment. "I've brought some for you anyway."

Mouthing a thank you to the staff, they slowly moved off.

Every time I sat with Shaz I would ask a question hoping for a response. It was a few months before I heard her voice.

I couldn't control my emotions. I was so elated. I was jumping out of my skin. *Shaz is breaking new ground. She's defying odds. She's proving the neurosurgeons and doctors wrong. What else is she capable of?*

The speech therapist trialled her with shapes, colours, numbers, and letters. "Sharyn can you point to the red card?" she asked.

We watched as she slowly moved her pointer finger towards the card. She wasn't always consistent and couldn't initiate, but it was clear some pathways in her brain were working.

An alphabet board was developed, enabling her to spell in response to a prompt or closed question.

"Shaz, can you spell Mum?" I asked as I sat beside her. "Shaz, can you spell Dad?" Whilst only small, she was making progress.

***

Things got even brighter when my brother, Phillip, and his partner Donna's first child was born.

My heart was overwhelmed with delight when we received the news.

"It's a boy," Mum announced as she put down the phone. "Donna and the baby are both doing well."

I sat in awe as I marvelled over what had just happened. *Who could have planned their first child being born on Sharyn's birthday? It's a miracle.*

After eight years, hope was springing back like green shoots emerging after a devastating fire. My brother lived two and a half hours away, but it wasn't going to stop us from visiting to meet his baby.

Watching the joy on everyone's face as they sat nursing the little bundle, I couldn't wait for my turn. I held him close studying his little features.

"Thank you, God," I whispered. "You're amazing and your timing is perfect."

They had brought this special gift into the world. A gift that meant more to us than anyone would ever know. He brought back life in the midst of our sadness; a sprinkle of hope and light in the darkness that overshadowed our existence.

***

A few years later we were celebrating another milestone.

The laws governing Compulsory Third Party Insurance differed from state to state. In some states CTP clicked in immediately. In Queensland, injured parties had to fight their cause. While Sharyn's accident occurred in NSW, her case came under Queensland's jurisdiction.

We were pushing Sharyn to our solicitor's office in the city. Mum wanted Jenny to see firsthand the catastrophic effects the accident had on Sharyn and understand who she was representing.

We were halfway across the road when we heard an almighty bang. The chair started to wobble; the pushing got harder. I looked down.

"Oh, no! We've just popped a tyre."

The traffic lights had changed so we were doing everything possible to get Sharyn safely to the other side. A stranger grabbed the chair from the front helping to pull her a little faster. Mum wasn't going to let a popped tyre get in her way, so we clunked our way to the office and home again with one wheel.

With the input of doctors, neurosurgeons, medical practitioners and therapists, Jenny worked on the case calculating what Sharyn would require for the remainder of her life.

Mum and I had dropped into her office to deliver some reports. Her large desk was empty contrasting with the boxes stacked from floor to ceiling along the walls.

My heart sank as she gave us the news.

"I'm going on maternity leave at the end of September."

Isn't this her third. This is never going to end?

I glanced at mum as I painted a smile and congratulated Jenny through gritted teeth.

She too was smiling, but I could see the exasperation in her eyes. She held onto her words until we entered the lift.

"Not again!" she said. "I can't believe it."

The frustration was still bubbling in her as we sat to have lunch with Susan, a long-term neighbour and friend.

"You need to contact the Legal Services Commission," Susan said as we sat sipping coffee in the mall. "They're an external body who deal with complaints."

Instant relief washed over Mum's face. "I had no idea such a body existed," she replied.

The waitress stood silently waiting to take our order.

"Can we have another five minutes, please?" Susan asked as we looked down at the menus. "We haven't stopped talking long enough to decide."

She gently nodded and headed to another table.

Mum was looking in a different direction to the menus.

"I wish I had known," she said as her attention turned back to the table. "We could've gone to them years ago. In the eleven years our solicitor has had two children and is about to go on maternity leave again."

Susan nearly spilt her tea. "Eleven years! That's ridiculous."

Mum phoned the Legal Services Commission the minute we arrived home. She was advised it could take up to eight weeks to resolve the complaint. Two days later our solicitor's firm called to arrange a meeting.

"We're terribly sorry for what has happened," the solicitor's representative said as he sat at the end of a large boardroom table, looking us straight in the eye. "I can't believe how much you've had to endure." His tone was compassionate and his address sincere.

Two other men, well-groomed and dressed in suits sat quietly on the other side of the table.

I was smiling politely, but I wasn't happy. *We've had enough. This has gone on for too long. We need help now.* I moved up a little in my chair, clasping my hands together. My heart was pumping so strongly I could feel it pulsing in my neck. My mouth was loaded like a gun ready to fire. I mustered up every ounce of energy and strength from within and assertively said.

"We've heard it all before." My head was shaking. "We've been here eleven years. I would like to know, what can you do for us? How are you going to do it? And what's your timeframe?"

I sat back in my chair surprised I had even spoken. I gritted my teeth to disguise how pleased I was as Mum usually did all the talking.

Mum glanced at me and whispered, "Where did that come from?"

Within a few weeks our case was escalated and we were heading towards negotiations with the other party.

***

The following night I heard Mum talking to the TV in the living room. "You can't be serious," she said. "They can't be... I can't believe this".

"Can't believe what?" I asked as I walked in. "What's happening?"

Mum's hands were shaking as much as her voice. "The Insurance company underwriting the third-party insurance in Sharyn's case has gone bust," she said. "It looks like everything is going to go pear shaped. Our hopes of settlement have just flown out the window."

"You're joking?" I replied, though I could hear in her voice she wasn't.

Her words were heavy. "We just started to get somewhere and now this," she said. "It's like a head injury. It's one step forward and two steps back, all the time."

I wanted to console her, but, how could I? *If only I had a magic wand and could fix everything.*

Relief refilled her cup a few weeks later when she was advised the case would proceed to its finality as the government of the day had stepped in and underwritten the now defunct company.

***

The day had finally arrived. Mum and I were sitting in the rear of the courtroom. My heart was beating faster than normal. I was holding my breath, not daring to move.

"How old is the mother?" the Supreme Court Judge asked as he lifted his head from the brief.

Our Queen's Council glanced back at Mum under his glasses. "Fifty-seven," she answered concisely.

I sat quietly wondering why he had asked about her age. *He must be assessing her capability to care for Sharyn.*

It was the only question he asked. His head returned to the brief, his hand moved across the desk and the document was stamped. Sharyn would be compensated for pain and suffering and loss of amenities of life, past loss of income, future economic loss, past gratuitous assistance and future care.

Not being able to hold on any longer Mum's tears started to flow. Her breaths were short, her long overdue sobs loud in the empty room.

My eyes were scanning the room wondering what was to happen next. I was searching my bag for a tissue, doing everything possible to hold it together.

It was rare to see Mum cry and I wasn't sure how to help. I kept whispering, "It's okay, it's over." My hand touched her arm.

We finally made it out of the courtroom. Everyone was quiet.

"I can't believe they have just put a price on my precious girl's life," she sobbed.

Standing like a statue… I watched… I waited… *Will Mum be okay? It's all come to the surface. It's been a long road.*

Mum eventually found her words. "Thank you," she said to the QC. "I'm so thankful it's finished."

The fresh air slowly filled my lungs, relieving the tension in my body as we stepped out onto the pavement.

"We need to go shopping," Mum said. "It's been a big day. You can have whatever you want."

I felt like someone had taken a full backpack off my back and I'd left it behind as we meandered up the mall. I'd lost ten kilos in an instant. The calculations of what Sharyn needed for the rest of her life, pushing to get things settled, and fearing she may not be adequately compensated were finally finished.

"Can I have some new undies and bras?" I asked as I skipped along. "Mine are so old and I hate forking out money to buy them."

Mum laughed, "Whatever you want."

We had four years reprieve before I felt the weight of the backpack again.

CHAPTER 18

The pace from being at home studying, meeting with the young people and caring for Shaz to working with two to three-year old children nearly killed me. I was on alert from the minute I arrived at the childcare centre. It was chaotic but I loved the children.

My role was filled with preparations and engaging children in activities, nappy changes, monitoring indoor and outdoor play, supervising meal times and cleaning.

After a few weeks I was exhausted. *If I just get through to lunchtime, I'll be okay. If I just get through the afternoon, I'll have a rest before getting Shaz.* I was running on empty ready to conk out at any time. I had nothing left in the tank and my resilience was low.

"Can you work five days?" The director asked as I stood monitoring the children on the playground. I gulped. *I'm not even keeping up with four. There's no way I can do five.*

"I'm not able to work Mondays," I replied. "I was clear about that when I started."

"It will be in your best interest to consider it," she responded in a firm tone. "We're finding it hard to cover the day."

I felt threatened, but I couldn't do it. I wouldn't survive.

Pulling out my work contract when I arrived home, I placed it in my handbag.

"I'm not able to work Mondays," I reiterated when I arrived the following morning. "I've signed a contract to work four days. That's all I can do."

She eased off for a time until I asked for two weeks leave.

"Jemima is on holidays during that time," she replied. "I've already approved her leave. I can only let one staff member have leave at a time. I won't have anyone to replace you."

My desire to return to the Solomon Islands to encourage the community who had been ravaged by violent conflict (locally referred to as 'the tensions') was stronger than keeping my job.

Two years earlier a group of militant youths from the island of Guadalcanal attacked settlements of islanders predominately from Malaita. The increasingly belligerent behaviour of these Guadalcanal militant groups resulted in some 25, 000 Malaitans fleeing.

The violence escalated at the start of 2000 when a resistance group named the Malaita Eagle Force (MEF), claiming to represent the interests of the Malaitans who had been displaced, armed themselves by raiding police armoires and subsequently took control of Honiara.

"You either replace me for two weeks, or replace me," I said to the director, putting my job on the line. "I'm booking my flight next week."

The Director glared at me. I didn't back down. The following week my leave was granted.

***

Things had changed significantly in the Solomon Islands since our previous trip. Their song had died, the locals were living in fear. A night curfew had been put in place.

A shiver went down my spine every time I heard a gunshot throughout the night. "Please keep us safe God," I prayed.

The following day we had gathered in the market place. Locals came from all directions. I was jittery. *If they're going to attack, a large group is an easy target. We're sitting ducks.*

My eyes constantly scanned the area. There was no way to tell who was who.

The scripture, 'You are near to the contrite and broken in heart,' rose to the forefront of my mind distracting me from the fear. "Help these people to know you are near, God" I prayed. "Restore hope and courage to their hearts."

That afternoon we were off on another adventure.

I dry reached every time I breathed. The slush under my feet was making my skin crawl. The flies so bad I was scared to open my mouth.

A small boy darted around the side of the hut. He was covered in dirt from head to toe. *How do these people survive in such squalid conditions?*

The locals had built an open frame church with a thatched roof on the side of a rubbish dump. Small wooden benches were dug into the dirt in rows.

Families displaced by the internal tension started to gather. I couldn't find words as I stood watching them lifting their hands and voices to God. *How do they do it? How do they find courage to praise God in such circumstances?*

The pastor stood up to read John 3:16. It was a verse I had heard so many times. My thoughts deepened as I listened to him reciting it in Pidgin.

His beaming smile amidst his darkened skin glistened like the sun on a lake. The smells, flies and concern for the people dissipated as I sought to interpret each word.

I was mesmerised by the love this group was showing towards these people. Heads were bowing in prayer as the musician played quietly in the background.

My body jumped as I felt something on my shoulder. I turned to find Peter standing with a young girl.

"Louise would like to give her heart to Jesus," he said. "Would you be happy to pray with her."

My thoughts flashed. *What if she can't understand me? What if I can't understand her? I need to get Julia one of the locals.*

The three of us bowed our knees in the dirt as Louise surrendered her life to God.

"Jesus, I believe you died on the cross for my sins," she prayed. "I'm sorry for the wrong things I've done. I ask you to forgive me. I ask you to come into my life and take full control."

I was in awe. *No place or person is too far from God, that he cannot reach.*

***

As I arrived back to Australia, I wondered if those thoughts would prove to be true.

Pressure from the director to work five days, continued to intensify as the year drew to a close. I kept digging my toes in, knowing my capacity couldn't stretch to five days. It would implicate my time supporting Shaz in the evenings. I had hoped to scale back to a five-day fortnight which wasn't an option until Nathan came to the centre.

Being high on the autistic spectrum, the childcare centre had been allocated funding to support him two days per week.

"That will be perfect," I said as the director offered me the role. "I would love to work with him."

At the same time my workload reduced, Peter and Angela invited me to join their family and a few others in seeking ways to reach out to their community and plant a new church in their area.

I didn't have to commit the decision to prayer as God had already been preparing my heart. Sirens had rung in my ears for weeks. My ears pricked up every time. *Is it an ambulance, police or fire truck?* At home, the shops, work, and church they rang. If it had been at the same place each time, I would have dismissed it as being near an ambulance station, but they followed me wherever I went.

What's going on? Why is this so constant? Something is seriously wrong.

Kneeling beside my bed I prayed, "God, the community needs you. People are lost, broken, disturbed. You're the only one who can heal them and restore hope."

Chapter 18 | Going Back

After a month of meeting together to pray, Peter was inspired to send out a Father's Day card. We all hit the streets sliding a card with a chocolate attached into the 450 letterboxes in the neighbourhood.

The following week we doorknocked the neighbours with a five-question survey.

"Do you think the Church has relevance in society?" I asked an elderly lady as she stood at the top of her stairs.

"I go to church when I catch the bus to town," she replied. "When I was a young girl I grew up in a convent," she continued. "I was very sad. A lovely nun would often bring me a little chocolate to brighten my day."

The questions were broad but would often bring out the person's beliefs and experiences.

We continued to pop a positive message into the mailboxes each week to encourage the community.

Peter and Angela started to collect the left-over bread and buns from the local bakery. The first night I did the delivery run, the hairs on my arms were standing on end.

The Husky's eyes were eerily clear and piercing. It was chained up but that didn't lower my heart rate. I didn't take my eyes off him as I shuffled towards the front door.

Mariah was oblivious to my fear.

"Would you like a cuppa?" she asked as she flicked on the kettle. As she shared her story expletives were flying everywhere. Her mouth was as marred as the cup she handed me.

Somehow in the midst, I felt at ease and that I was in the centre of God's will. *Jesus sat with people like Mariah. He loved them and gave his life for them.*

A few weeks later, Peter and Angela invited the neighbours to enjoy an Aussie barbeque in their backyard. Steak sizzled; salads lined the tables as the smell of cooked onions filled the air.

Music played in the background as neighbours chatted and children played.

As the plates were gathered, Tony the guest speaker sat on the stool ready to share his story. Neighbours were sitting scattered around the edges of the marquee. Silence settled upon the group as he started to speak.

Faces were sombre as he talked about his marriage being at breaking point.

"I was overcome," he said. "I didn't know what to do. A friend of mine had organised a hotel room for me to stay, I was numb as I sat staring at the coffee table, until a red book caught my eye."

"As I picked it up," he continued, "a small sticky note was hanging out. The verse struck me as I opened the page. My heart broke."

> In the same way, husbands ought to love their wives as their own bodies. He who loves his wife loves himself. After all, no one ever hated their own body, but they feed and care for their body, just as Christ does the church. Ephesians 5:28-29.

"I bowed my head," he continued, "and asked God to forgive me for any damage I had caused my wife."

As I glanced around, I noticed tears welling up in one of the lady's eyes. *His story has obviously struck a chord. I must catch up with her later.*

"I pleaded with Him to restore my marriage," Tony continued. "Peace engulfed me as I wept. I was changed that day. The road back wasn't easy, but my wife and I are still together."

The silence lingered when he finished. Peter extended a hand to pray for him and encouraged anyone who wanted prayer to let him know.

It wasn't long before everyone pitched in to clean up.

"Do you know anyone who owns a donkey?" Peter asked as we stacked the chairs.

My imagination ran faster than a horse frightened by a car backfiring. I started to laugh.

"I know a few donkeys," I replied, "but I don't know anyone who owns one."

Peter continued to roll with the jokes.

I was doubled over. My face was red. I could hardly breathe.

Angela was laughing as Peter grinned from ear to ear. It wasn't possible to take him seriously, but I knew he was. I eventually regained my composure, enough for the words to spill out.

"Why are you looking for a donkey?" I asked.

"We're going to run a Palm Sunday Festival, in the sports park," he replied. "We want to create a re-enactment of Jesus' triumphant entry into Jerusalem. A local church has offered us their costumes, we have palm branches, we just need a donkey and someone to ride it."

"Good luck," I replied as I continued to chuckle.

I nearly fell over the chairs when he asked me if I could face paint.

"I've never done it before," I said as I regained my balance. "I can give it a go."

"Check with some of the young people from church," he replied. "Felicity will be able to help you too."

The stories of Peter trying to find a donkey had us in stitches for days. He managed to find one for the afternoon and persuaded a young man from the community to ride it.

It was very entertaining and made it to the front page of the local paper. The face painting was a different story.

"Would you like your face painted?" I asked one of the boys who had arrived early with his parents to set up."

He chose a batman face from the book and sat in front of me ready to go.

My hand was shaking. *It can't be too hard. Just follow the outline.*

I was making a mess. I didn't know how to fix it. Eventually I splashed a little more paint on and showed him in the mirror. He looked like he was going to cry.

"What is that?" he asked.

How do I respond? "I think I need Felicity to fix it a little," I replied. I called her over.

She took one look at the child's face and glared at me.

"What have you done?" she gasped.

I didn't know whether to laugh or cry. "Can you fix it for me please? I'm going to find Bianca. We need help."

Deciding to stay away from the paint, I entertained the children while they were waiting in line.

Five hundred people streamed in throughout the afternoon to enjoy the food and entertainment.

As the sun went down, we started the evening program. Stars twinkled above in the cloudless sky as families sat on the grass listening to the band.

The atmosphere hushed as Paul stepped forward to present the good news of the Gospel. His voice was clear in the crisp air.

> Romans 3:23 says, for all have sinned and fall short of the glory of God, and all are justified freely by His grace through the redemption that came by Christ Jesus.

Thinking about the first time Jan and Leila came to our home and spoke about redemption. peace and joy bubbled up inside of me. *I can't believe how much my life has changed since that day.* I whispered a prayer thanking God and asking Him to reveal Himself to others as He had to me.

***

A few months later with only a small team, we started to hold our Sunday morning celebrations at the sports club. As we continued reaching out to the community, we became increasingly aware that people were spiritually indifferent and apathetic to the Gospel.

It took months before the new church started to grow.

CHAPTER 19
The Open Door

Eyes were looking at me from every direction as I walked towards the bus stop. Feeling uneasy, I started to fiddle wondering if a button on my top had popped. My mind was scurrying until the obvious hit me. *I'm a foreigner.*

A smile returned to my face as I relaxed. After travelling to the Solomon Islands five times on short term mission trips, the door had opened for me to return for an extended period.

The decision wasn't easy. Whilst I had many adventures, they were short term as I wanted to come home and help with Shaz. When my job contract ended, my longing to go and live among the people was stronger than wanting to stay. The struggle had intensified within me. *If I don't go now and the door shuts, I'll always regret it.*

Giving myself to helping wherever I could; I served in the kindergartens in town and up in the village, the centre caring for children with disability and the church on the rubbish dump.

I had become so used to their way of life I had forgotten I stood out.

Carolina greeted me at the bus stop. "I heard how you helped Mosese, when you were up in the village," she said, "his daughter's still wearing your shirt."

My eyes caught hers as my mind stuttered. *The village is in the middle of nowhere. How on earth did you hear about that?*

We had been walking back from the village kindy when I noticed Mosese lying on the side of the road. Blood was gushing out of his leg, like water from a broken pipe.

I stepped away trying not to vomit. Reality was screaming in my head. *It's forty minutes to the river and another forty to town. There are no trucks coming through as the roads are too damaged. He's going to die!*

Adrenaline kicked in. I took off my shirt covering my dress and tied it as a tourniquet.

Mosese drawn eyes looked at me. "You're going to ruin your shirt."

"It's just a shirt," I replied as I tied it to his leg. *Your life is on the line.*

Hearing the trees rustling I looked up to find four men clambering towards us with a makeshift stretcher.

Hoisting him on they ran off down the road.

Noticing his leg dangling off the stretcher I ran after them shouting, "Lift his leg, lift his leg up."

As they stopped to reposition him, I handed them a bottle of water. "He'll need this."

I could hardly breath as I walked towards the little house where I was staying. I sat frozen unable to move as the shock of what had just happened caught up with me. Staring at the thatched walls my thoughts turned to Sharyn who would have been lying unconscious on the side of the road after her accident. I thanked God for the first responders and prayed for Mosese. "Please help him to survive God."

The following day we received news Mosese had made it. A truck carrying cargo was bogged a few miles down the road. The men helped to pushed it out, turned it around and raced him to the hospital. Mosese had survived and so did the shirt.

***

When I returned home, I stayed with mum for a few days, waiting for the tenants to move from my unit. Caring for Sharyn on her own whilst working full time had taken its toll on her. A day never passed without her spending time with Shaz.

Chapter 19 | The Open Door

I knew it was time for me to step up again and returning to work was imminent. Shaz seemed just the same as I dropped in to see her. Six months had gone by but nothing much had changed.

The new church had also grown from fifteen to fifty people and was buzzing. "If you want church growth," I said to Peter and Angela jokingly, "you'll have to send me back to the Solomon Islands."

"We'd like to keep you here," Peter responded. "Would you be interested in a pastoral assistant role two days per week?"

My mind was ticking. *I won't have the rent from my unit when I move back in. I'll need an income. But it's not about the money.*

"Can I have a few days to consider it?" I replied.

I thought about the offer. *I was serving voluntarily before I left. The community is only fifteen minutes away. I'll have plenty of time to help Shaz. To be paid two days a week isn't unreasonable. I'll accept the offer.*

***

Slotting back in I helped with the bread run, teaching Religious Instruction, helping with children's church, and any other opportunity that came my way.

Giving my time and resources to serve the community was fulfilling. I met people from all walks of life, different professions and different values. I particularly enjoyed working with the children, encouraging them and inspiring them to be all they could be.

It became clear over time many from the community were struggling with addictions and the effects of making wrong life decisions. Their choices impacted their relationships, their finances and their employment capacity. Some found ways of restoration whilst others continued to cycle through their habits.

Mum and I returned to bringing Shaz home of an evening to give her a change of environment and time with the family.

Finding it hard to say no to opportunities and caring for Shaz and other people with complex issues, fatigued had started to set in.

"I'm not here," I would say to the phone, refusing to pick it up when it rang. Ducking and weaving became another habit as people walked towards me at church. *Not today. I'm empty.*

As the year was coming to an end my thoughts plagued me. *I can't keep functioning like this. Something's got to give. I'll give up everything but I don't want to let go of my work in the school.*

Finding a nannying job, I resigned from my pastoral assistant role. My energy bounced back and my capacity slowly returned as I cared for Hayley, Stephanie, and Michael. They were full of life and fun and became a great source of joy.

My brother and his partner had another two girls who also brightened my world. From a young age they would come to Brisbane for holidays. Not having had my own children I treasured every moment with them. They embraced Shaz easily, not having known her any other way.

"Can we have one pleeease?" they would ask as they sat staring at the cream buns we had collected for the bread run.

"Yes, you can," I replied, "as soon as we've finished." Every time we stopped at another house; they would look at the packet hoping it was the last delivery.

Holidays became my highlight. We rollerbladed, went go-karting, took Shaz bowling, and spent hours playing monopoly.

***

As a few of us from the church continued serving in the school, chaplaincy came up in conversation.

"I'm happy to do the groundwork," I said to Peter, "and support the role in the school."

I simplified the piles of paperwork and drafted an outline of what was required. The process of establishing a local chaplaincy committee, raising sufficient funds to support the role and to get the school P&C on board took about eight months.

A number of people encouraged me to apply, but fears I didn't have the capacity haunted me. *I'm feeling much better but what if I end up back where I was?*

Meeting with a minister from the local chaplaincy committee I shared my journey of caring for Shaz, and others I had come into contact with over the years through the new church. She nodded as I listed my concerns.

Chapter 19 | The Open Door

"I've got just the right course for you," she said as she stood up and walked towards the room beside us.

As she returned, she handed me a brochure on a clinical pastoral education course. "I did this many years ago," she continued. "It helped me to establish good working boundaries and develop other great skills."

I saw it as a sign. I made enquires, enrolled in the course and applied for the Chaplaincy job.

The job interview was going well until Chris the school principal asked me a question I didn't know how to answer. Making up a few words I started to ramble before realising I was completely off track. I stopped. Looking back at him I asked, "What was the question again?"

He smiled before repeating it.

A few days later I was offered the position. "You did well in the interview," Chris said as he congratulated me.

Lifting my eyebrows, I replied, "Even when I couldn't answer the question?"

His face was bright as he responded. "Humour goes a long way."

I chuckled. *Little did he know, I wasn't trying to be funny.*

The chaplaincy role increased the church's capacity to support the school community. Walking alongside children like Lucas was really satisfying.

Lucas was often waiting at the school gate when I arrived.

"Can I carry your box?" he'd ask with outstretched arms.

He'd chat away about all sorts of things as we headed to the office.

"You must be a great help to your Mum," I said one day as I passed the box over the fence.

His head dropped as he murmured, "My Mum's dying of Cancer."

My heart broke. I was speechless. I wanted to wrap him up in my arms, though even a hug wouldn't be appropriate. I kept a special eye out for him and often asked how he was going.

The months ahead were filled with providing a listening ear to teachers, students and their families. We established lunchtime programs to engage children who were struggling socially and made connections with the wider community to engage their support.

I was in the role about eight months when the bombshell was dropped.

***

"I'm taking six months long service," Peter said as we walked towards the school car park.

His words didn't register until the following day.

"Angela's coming with me," he said.

The words reverberated in my ears. I was shattered. As I was trying to maintain my calm a few words trickled out of my mouth.

"Yes, of course." I murmured. "That's great."

Calculating the impact of them both leaving overwhelmed me. I was still trying to come to terms with reality a week later when another missile was fired.

"Did you know Chris is taking a twelve month break next year?" Peter asked.

"No, I didn't." I stammered.

Waves of sadness pummelled me like the ocean waves on a windy day. There was no one to rescue me. I had to find my feet. I had to stay afloat. I had to believe it would all work out.

I couldn't take anymore, but there was more to come.

Ivan, one of our Religious Instruction teachers was standing in the under covered area at school after our lessons finished.

"I'm not going to be able to teach RI next year," he said. "I'll try to find a replacement, but I can't do it."

"You'll have to take a ticket and get in the line," I replied jokingly. "Everyone's leaving, you'll have to wait your turn." I was smiling but internally I was drowning. Making light of the comment was the only way I could keep myself afloat.

I yearned to leave, too, but what about the children?

CHAPTER 20
A Steady Force

"Stand firm; don't let anything easily move you. Always give yourself to the work of the Lord, knowing your labour is not in vain," shouted at me from the page as I sat reading the Bible.

My fists were clenched, I was shaking my head. *I'm not standing firm, everything's moving. Everyone's going. I want to go, too.*

As the words absorbed deeper into my mind, I knew my time at the school wasn't finished. I felt sad, lost, and alone, but I had to trust God.

I sat in the office with one of the leaders from my chaplaincy committee, wading through what I could manage and what needed to be put on hold. Over the coming months I gathered new helpers and slowly rebuilt my programs.

My emotions heaved when the next wave hit.

During his leave Peter made the decision to step back from his church leadership role.

Steven and Andrew who were part of the leadership team had worked hard to keep everything functioning in Peter's absence. They both had young families and worked full time in managerial roles.

"Christine and I won't be continuing next year," Andrew said to the leadership team as we gathered to discuss the future of the church. "My workload is increasing and I don't have the capacity."

Steven and his wife Clara, took up the reins intermittently to stabilise the church as we sought direction for the way forward.

After a season of praying and seeking for a new minister – without success – the church decided to cease its role in the community.

I felt sad. I had poured so much of my life into supporting the new church and now it was gone. The sadness would shift to anger as I watched everyone move on whilst I stood left to carry the load at the school.

My dad's words spoken years earlier were counselling me as I sat on my bedroom floor. *Only you can make the decision and you're responsible for the outcome.*

I thought about all that had transpired over the five years. *I believe God called me. I'm not sorry. It's been worth it.*

***

Over the next few months, I attended a number of services with a friend, Debbie, to find a new place to worship.

"I'd like to come back to this church again," Debbie said one morning. "I felt really welcome here. The message encouraged me, too."

Her words were like music to my ears. She didn't go to church regularly, though she was open to spiritual things. Her response was a good indicator of how the congregation embraced visitors.

The church seemed to be right for me, too. The little community had similar values and gave me room to find healing and recovery, without any expectation to serve. The congregation were long term supporters of school chaplaincy, which was an added bonus.

Jill the interim principal replacing Chris, was supportive of my role in the school and Lilly, the deputy principal, remained a steady force. Members of my chaplaincy committee continued to encourage me, helping me to reshape the way ahead.

I had been working closely with a young student, Theresa, for a number of months. She was only eight though always at the centre of incidents in the school and often found herself at the principal's office.

Chaper 20 | A Steady Force

Time was structured in the school each week for me to spend time with her though I was often called to give her some time out to give the teachers and other students a reprieve.

"Would you like to help me set up for Supa Club?" I asked as I collected her from the office. "You can fill the treasure box."

Her eyes always sparkled as she sifted through the prizes I had collected for the program. I often gave her a challenge encouraging better behaviour with the incentive of picking one if she followed through.

Another incentive was attending Kids' Club on a Friday night. Her mother Cadence allowed me to take her and put it in place as a reward. Cadence was on her own with three other children so it gave her a small break.

Theresa enjoyed the interaction with the leaders and other children from the community and it gave me the opportunity to check on the rest of her family when I collected her.

I had noticed Theresa's behaviour escalating throughout the term and Cadence stress levels were increasing.

"Something's going to give," I said to Lilly, the deputy principal out of concern. "They need a break from each other. I could house Theresa over the holidays. It would settle everything down and her transition back to school will be easier."

Lilly wasn't opposed to the idea though she encouraged me to seek advice from Mandy my district coordinator before continuing.

"If you house a child from your school," Mandy said, "you'll be instantly dismissed."

I couldn't take the risk so I let the idea go.

When I heard arrangements were made for Theresa to travel interstate to stay with her father over the holidays, I breathed a sigh of relief. *At least it's a break, for all of them.*

***

I was taken by surprise when Cadence rang me a few weeks later on the first day of the school holidays. Her words were rolling together without a breath. "I can't cope with the other children," she said. "I need help. I'm suicidal."

"Just put the phone down," I said calmly. "Bring the children and come to my house."

"I will only have the boys," Cadence replied. "Kiely is at day care."

After rustling up some food I pulled a few games out of the cupboard.

"Would you like something to eat?" I asked as they arrived. "I'm just having my breakfast."

The boys were sitting at the table before I had finished the sentence. They munched through the cereal like they hadn't eaten for a week.

Offering them a chocolate milk I looked for the largest glasses in the cupboard.

"Anyone for toast?"

"I've set a few things up in the other room," I said as they eventually stopped chewing. "Would you like to have a game while mum and I have a quick chat?"

Cadence's mind was still racing. Her words took up every inch of space in my brain. "The boys are continually fighting and don't stop asking me for things," she said. "I can't take them out as I can't even put food on the table. I can't do it anymore."

My head was spinning. I occasionally glanced to check on the boys to grab a moment of reprieve.

She eventually stopped as she looked at her watch.

"I have a doctor's appointment at 12:00pm," she said. "We need to get going soon."

"Why don't you leave the boys with me?" I replied. "I can take care of them for a couple of hours."

"I want to go with Mum," Derby the eldest said as he appeared from nowhere.

"What about you, Conner?" I asked as he slowly walked into the room. "I'm going to the shops, if you would like to come."

His cheeky grin and sparkling eyes told me it was a yes.

We were just walking back in the door when the phone rang.

Chaper 20 | A Steady Force

"They're admitting me into hospital," Cadence said through short breaths. "child safety will be coming to collect Conner."

My hand went over my mouth as my mind shot straight to her little one in day care. My heart was racing but I managed to keep my mind calm.

"I'll come and collect Derby from the hospital," I responded. "child safety can pick the boys up from my place."

The minute the words left my mouth I turned. Fear had already gripped Conner's eyes.

I wanted to tell him it'll be okay. *But will it?*

Taking hold of my nerves to stay strong I calmly said, "Mum has to go to hospital for a couple of days. We need to go and collect Derby."

We were guided to a small room on arrival. Cadence's eyes were swollen. Conner ran across the room, wrapped his arms around her and wouldn't let go.

The crack in my heart widened as he started to cry.

"Child safety will come and collect the children," the social worker said in a monotone voice. "I can't tell you how long it will take to find somewhere for them to stay. There's no guarantee the children will stay together, either."

Derby was standing with his arms folded rocking back and forth.

They can't separate them, I screamed inside. *The little one's only three.*

Mandy, my district coordinators words rang in my head as I scrambled for a solution. *"If you house a child from your school, you'll be instantly dismissed."*

This is different isn't it? It's an emergency.

CHAPTER 21
Am I Gone

"I'll take them," I said as I clasped my hands. "I'm not supposed to. I'll deal with my job later."

Cadence's shoulders dropped. "We'll be able to visit you," I said. "If you give me your key, I'll collect some of the children's gear. I'll need you to ring the childcare centre and give them permission for me to collect Kiely."

Conner was screaming.

"It's only for a couple of days," I said to reassure him. "We can come back and see mum tomorrow."

Derby walked over and took his hand. "It's better if we stay together," he said bravely.

The boys settled quite easily in the evening. Their computer game took their minds off the day. Kiely drifted off to sleep in the company of her brothers.

Sitting at the desk I tried to work through how I was going to negotiate the holidays with three extra children in my care and Shaz; then there was my employer.

Should I let them know? I'll be in trouble if they find out and I haven't told them. I'll be in trouble if I do tell them. Better to be safe than sorry, or is it?

I flicked off an email.

The following day was tough. Conner had been bellowing since we left the hospital. I pulled the car over and turned to him.

"I know you're sad," I said, "I know you don't want to leave Mum."

His yelling dropped a few decibels.

"Would you like to come back and see Mum tomorrow?"

He nodded.

As I moved the car back onto the road, he started again.

I edged the car to the curb. After the third attempt I turned the car off.

"I can't drive while you're screaming," I said calmly, "it's not safe. We're going to have to sit here for half an hour to give you time to calm down."

Derby was now yelling. "Shut up, Conner! We don't want to sit here for half an hour."

Looking back at Derby I said, "It's not about you Derby, it's not about Conner. It's about all of us. We need to make it home safely."

Conner started to quieten.

"Do you think you'll be okay?" I asked. "If you can stop crying, we can go."

His sad eyes looked back at me as he gave me another nod.

I restarted the car and swallowed a mouthful of fresh air that had blown in the window. I pulled back onto the road. *Here's hoping.*

We made it through the day. I was almost out of energy as I sat down at the desk. The children were bunkered down for the night.

Fear gripped me as I opened my emails. The red flag on an email from my district coordinator put me on alert. My eyes quickly scanned the page.

> You need to be at head office first thing Monday morning.
> Doug, the field director needs to see you.

There was no room to think about the meeting until Sunday night. *I need to stay calm for the children's sake. There's no way I can trudge them all into the city. I'm going to have to put it off.*

I sent Mandy a text.

Chapter 21 | Am I Gone

> I'm unable to attend the meeting with Doug tomorrow. The children are still with me.

It bought me some time, but I didn't realise cancelling would make things worse. A reply came the following day.

> Doug's not happy, Mandy wrote. He didn't receive my email until he arrived at the office. He wouldn't have come in if he'd known as his wife was home sick.

My heart was pounding as I read every word, but I dismissed it quickly. *I can't deal with it today. I've got enough on my plate.*

***

Cadence was released from hospital a week later just before school went back. The boys stayed with me until Sunday to give her a chance to transition.

Feeling sick in the pit of my stomach I arrived at head office the following day to front Doug. My body was shaking as I stood in front of the mirror in the toilets.

Don't look down. Maintain eye contact. Keep your shoulders back and have your tissues ready.

Doug was sitting behind his desk as I entered the room. Mandy was standing staring out the window.

I took a deep breath and said, "Good morning."

Doug's face was already bright red. "You were given a directive and you didn't follow it," he said as he sat like a king on his throne. Silence fell over the room.

My tongue was on the roof of my mouth. My lips held tightly closed.

"If something happened and it made the media, we would all be sunk," he continued.

My eyebrows furrowed. *Media. That's extreme. Why would it hit the media?*

"You have a lack of submission to authority," he continued.

In the midst of the stress I wanted to laugh. *You've got to be kidding me. Who are you? I have spent the last seven years learning about authority and submission.*

I was caught off guard when he fired the last bullet. "If you want to continue in your chaplaincy role, we'll have to put you under a six months diminished performance review."

My defences were up. I was wringing my hands. I bit my tongue, but I couldn't contain the words firing up within me.

"One of those children was sitting in the Mental Health Ward with their mother for hours," I said in a strong tone. "The children were going to be separated from her and potentially each other. The little one's only three. I couldn't stand by and watch them get ripped apart when I knew I could do something."

His response shocked me. "The staff wouldn't have gone home without finding someone to look after them," he replied. "Even if they were split up, they would have been provided for and kept safe."

I sat staring at him, like I was looking at a dead fish that had just washed up on the beach. I knew it would go against me if I argued.

"Mandy will go through the diminished performance review," he continued. "I'll give you a week to decide."

My heart was heavy as I looked at the pages. *They're going to scrutinise everything I do in the school, when I haven't done anything wrong.*

Tears welled up in my eyes as I looked back at him. "I don't want to give up my job," I said, "I'll do whatever it takes."

The diminished performance review required me to meet with the principal of the school every week.

"Hi Jill," I said to the acting principal as I popped my head into her room. "I'm here for the meeting."

She gave me an inquisitive look. "What meeting?"

"To discuss the diminished performance review," I replied. "I'm supposed to check in with you each week."

She glanced over the form. "Just tick the box," she said as she handed it back to me.

My eyes narrowed as I stood staring at the form. I was relieved but anxiety kept troubling my mind. *What if someone checks? She won't know what I've done. It could get me into greater trouble.*

Chapter 21 | Am I Gone

After the same response the following week, I just ticked the box. After all Jill authorised it.

Whilst Jill was relaxed about the process, I was struggling deep within. I didn't believe what I had done was wrong in fact I thought the opposite. *I kept the children together; they were able to access their own clothes and visit their mum daily. They had a good holiday and Cadence was released from hospital earlier than expected.*

My nerves got the better of me a few weeks later and I thought it was all going to end.

I was standing at the counter of the school office signing out when Lilly – the deputy principal popped her head around the corner.

"Are you going now?" she asked. "I'll walk you to your car."

I froze as her words hit my ears. I was holding back the tears. "If I've lost my job, you can tell me here. You don't need to walk me to my car."

Jill was now at her door. She looked at Lilly standing next to me. "I'll come, too," she said.

My heart sank. I looked back at them with sorrow in my eyes. "Please just tell me, am I gone?"

"You haven't lost your job," Lilly replied. "Just come with us."

My heart was pounding louder than my feet on the steps. "My car's this way." I said as I signalled with my hand.

"Can you follow us for a minute?" Jill called as she walked towards another vehicle. She lifted the boot. "We're amazed how you gave up your time and housed Cadence children on the holidays. We know you've taken money out of your own pocket to feed them."

I looked down at the beautiful pink basket full of groceries in the boot. My tears turned into sobs as I let go of all of the fear, and anxiety that had built up in my heart.

"You might need one of these," Lilly said as she opened the box of tissues sitting on the top.

The silky texture in my hand reminded me of the five-star hotels I'd stayed in when I worked in the travel industry.

"These are amazing," I said as I rubbed them on my nose and inhaled the clean, pleasant smell of eucalyptus. "Where did you get these from?"

"The supermarket," Lilly replied. "They're three ply."

A smile had returned to my face. "I need to invest in some of these," I said. "I can't believe I didn't know they existed."

It wasn't long before I needed them again.

CHAPTER 22
Bussed In

A shiver went down my spine as helicopters hovered above. A line of army officers walked side by side combing the area.

"This is devastating," I said to Claire as I glanced at what looked like a war zone. Trees were uprooted, houses and debris were scattered across paddocks and cars were upturned and suspended in trees. My heart started pounding as we stopped at the police roadblock.

Claire and I were in a camp with young people on the Sunshine Coast when we first heard the news. The program had been reworked as it had been raining torrentially for three days.

"We've been instructed to get the young people out first thing in the morning," our Camp Director said. "The rivers are rising. We're at risk of getting cut off."

"There won't be time for breakfast," he continued. "We'll pack food for everyone."

The leader's faces were pale. They had seen the footage of people on rooftops awaiting rescue, whilst the rapidly flooding waters engulfed the town ten minutes from where they lived.

My heart was moved as one of the strapping farmers prayed.

"They're praying for us," he said as his voice quivered. "We need to be praying for them."

Everything was surreal when we arrived home. The sun was shining brightly in the sky void of clouds. You couldn't even tell it had rained where I lived, yet houses were poking up out of a sea of brown water across many suburbs.

Three young girls stayed with me until roads were made clear for them to get home. I had driven out to one of the worst hit areas to help Claire with her children when she invited me to the recovery centre.

A man sitting at the table caught my eye as we walked in. His eyes were vacant as he sat alone, hunched over an empty cup. His head shook ever so slightly as someone offered him a sandwich.

The kitchen was buzzing as a team of ladies chopped fruit and vegetables, and prepared meals for the locals, volunteers and recovery workers. I kept my head down as they talked amongst themselves.

"It's the fifth funeral in two days," one of the ladies said. "I'm not sure how everyone's going to get through this."

My heart cried every time I heard or read a story. We had been through our own trauma when Sharyn was injured, but I had never experienced such a magnitude of community devastation. The community had been completely and utterly smashed as the unprecedented heavy rain and flooding had turned into a powerful inland tsunami.

Claire and I took a short break from the kitchen. As we sat at a table with a couple of local ladies, the stories kept flowing. I wasn't sure where to look. I didn't know what to say. No words would be adequate at a time like this.

The atmosphere in the recovery tent was solemn. As I discreetly glanced around, people's eyes were glazed; their faces were pale, they looked drained and exhausted.

In the evening the community gathered to pray. Voices shook as they prayed for people who were still missing, families who had lost loved ones, and for those who had lost their homes.

I could only whisper, "Have mercy, Lord."

Chapter 22 | Bussed In

I travelled out to help Claire a number of times before heading back to my school for the pupil free day.

"I've received an email from Sonya, a past teacher," Lilly said. "Her brother and sister-in-law have children at the school in the area that has been devastated by the floods. They're trying to organise school shoes for all of the children before they return."

For a moment I was too stunned to say anything.

"I've been out there," I replied. "It's devastating. We need to do something. I'll give Sonya a call."

The day was busy attending meetings and going through student lists with the teachers. My mind wondered how children who had lost everything would cope with returning to school.

"They've already arranged the shoes," Lilly said as I arrived back at the office.

My eyes widened as I looked back at her.

"Wow, that was quick," I replied.

"They want to start a breakfast program," she continued. "A lot of families have been relocated. The children will have to leave early to be bussed in to school each day."

My mind was ticking. I was trying to find a way to help. "We could give them our resources?" I replied. "There'll be such a demand for supplies from the food bank we should probably put our breakfast program on hold for the moment. It would help them get started."

I arranged to take the supplies to the school and meet Theresa, Sonya's sister-in-law when I arrived. The hour and a half drive from Brisbane was scenic as the landscape along the highway changed from city buildings to open spaces.

The atmosphere in the school was chaotic. Theresa's phone was ringing constantly. Parents were sorting supplies scattered all over the room. People were coming and going.

I stood back trying to stay out of the way.

"Would you like some help in the morning?" I asked Theresa. "I'm staying overnight so I can pop back early."

She took a deep breath. "That would be great," she replied, a sound of relief in her voice. "I'll be here about eight o'clock."

The verandah was noisy as children clamoured to fill their plates with cereal and grab a flavoured milk. Parents were stepping over them trying to get to the office. Milk was splattered everywhere.

"We might need to put a few systems in place for tomorrow," I said to Theresa as I gathered the bowls and cups left scattered as the children headed to class.

She lifted her eyebrows in agreement.

"We're having an emergency relief meeting at 9:00am today," she replied. "You're welcome to join us."

I followed her down the stairs to where the parents had gathered. I stood quietly and smiled as I was introduced.

Carly, the principal, was charismatic. Her face was animated despite all that had gone on. She lived in the schoolhouse next door and was on the ground the minute the devastation unfolded.

The school was on the hill and became a refuge for families and their pets as they sought higher ground. Her strength, resilience and focus on recovery were obvious.

"We have a guidance officer in each classroom," she said to reassure the parents. "They're available to support the children whenever needed. The trauma counsellors will be here next week and will be assessing each child."

"A lot of resources are flooding into the school," she continued. "We need to put a wish list together and develop priorities to support the learning needs of the children. It's important for us to rebuild a stable environment so the emotional impact on the children can gradually be addressed."

I stepped forward offering to scribe as Carly's phone rang. Ideas were flowing quicker than I could write. Each one was discussed and categorised into high need, moderate need, and if possible.

As Carly talked about the services being made available at the recovery centre next door, my pulse started to jump. *Now is a good time to offer our help. I hope it doesn't offend anyone.*

"Whilst you're talking about support," I said sheepishly, "my school is open to me coming and helping for a couple of days each week. They'll cover my wages. They want to support the recovery wherever they can."

There was no movement. Eyes were looking back at me like I had just wrapped a baby up and comforted it in my arms. Mist was forming in their eyes. No one spoke.

Carly finally broke the silence. "That would be wonderful," she said. "It will be a great help to have an extra set of hands around the place."

"I agree," Theresa responded. "My sister-in-law has done nothing but praise the work Nyree has done in her school."

Now tears were forming in my eyes. I was overwhelmed that they had opened the door to allow me to walk with them through the painful journey of recovery. It didn't take long to realise; this wasn't the worst of it.

***

A few months later the children were huddled under the school building. We were doing everything to keep them quiet and settle their nerves.

"Let's make them sandwiches and a drink," I said to one of the staff.

An hour had gone by and we were still waiting. Rain had started to fall turning the track at the back of the recovery tent into sludge.

Carly finally emerged.

"He's here," she said, clasping her hands in excitement. "Remember children, best manners."

Security officers lined the fence as the children trudged past. The community devastated by the floods were sandwiched in like sardines. I stood at the back, leaving room for others.

As the music started the children lined up just as they had practised. They stood with their hands clasped, waiting for the cue from the drama teacher to begin. Their faces lit up as they welcomed the Duke of Cambridge with their song.

Prince William was casually dressed and wore the beaming smile he carries on every media page. He let out a chuckle as one of the children dressed like a kangaroo jumped across the platform in the middle of their Aussie drama purposefully created for him.

"Thank you," he said as he bent over to speak with them. "That was fantastic."

The children stood mesmerised by the hype.

As they arrived back at the school excitement broke out. They were chatting and jumping around like they had just returned from winning a grand final in football. It was impossible to quieten them as they waited for their parents to arrive.

Prince William was one of the many dignitaries and visitors who came to the school bringing gifts and messages of hope to the children. Every day was brightened, but the constant interruptions made it hard to rebuild structure and normality.

The school welcomed the disruption in the early part of the year, believing the opportunities would build positive memories for years to come.

For Dale, we didn't know how he would ever return to normality. He hadn't just lost his home he had lost three family members. Clinging to a tree hoping to be rescued he saw the ravaging floods unfold.

Dale had a staff member with him from the moment he arrived at school and was allowed to keep a friend with him at all times.

Our only directive from the trauma counsellors was to keep him in the school and keep him safe. His trauma was so great, he couldn't sit still for more than a minute, he struggled to eat and at times would explode with aggression.

Despite suffering a tragedy, greater than most humans would endure in a lifetime, Dale had a fantastic sense of humour.

"Mrs Moffatt (Carly) there's a delivery at the front door for you," I said loud enough for Dale to hear me.

She dismissed me with her eyes.

I looked back at her and signalled with my hand, pointing at the door.

"It's pretty big and heavy. I'd bring it in, but I can't lift it."

She realised we were up to something and played along. "I'm not expecting anything," she said as she headed towards the entry. "Wow, it's a big one!"

"I think you'll get a great surprise," I continued as I tapped on the box. "Why don't you open it?"

Before she could lift the flap, Dale popped his head up. "Surprise!"

She placed her hand over her mouth as her eyes widened.

"Oh, what a precious gift!" she exclaimed. "It's the best, ever! What am I going to do with it?" She gave Dale a hug as he climbed out of the box.

Dale's smile lit up the whole school.

"That was so much fun," he said. "Can we do it again?"

"Not today," I replied. "Mrs Moffatt will be on to us, maybe one day when she's not expecting it."

***

One day I took my eyes off him for a moment and he was gone.

"Have you seen Dale?" I said to Cameron the music therapist. He had been with him five minutes earlier.

"No," he replied. "I thought he was with you."

Panic pulsated through my body. I was running down the stairs. "Check the playground," I called. "I'll check the road."

"Have you seen Dale?" I asked one of the older boys under the building, "we can't find him."

He shook his head.

"Run and tell Mrs Moffatt he's missing."

My breath was tight, but I managed to call his name as I ran up and down the street. Other voices were calling from inside the school.

I put my hands in the air and shook my head. Cameron did the same from across the playground.

"We're going to have to call his dad," I said as we headed back to the office.

CHAPTER 23
The Garden

"Dale's in the 4/5 classroom," one of the boys called as I ran up the stairs. I relaxed the minute I lay eyes on him. Oblivious to the search party looking for him, Dale showed me a tower of blocks he had been working on.

"Next time you're going to run away," I said to him jokingly, "Can you let me know first?"

His broad cheeky grin splashed across his face as he turned back to what he was doing.

"Can you watch him for a minute?" I said to Cameron as I rolled my eyes, "I need some water."

As I headed out the door, I ran into a parent.

"I was looking for you," she said. "I want to thank you for the program you're doing with my girls."

A gentle smile crossed my face as my mind ticked. *Which program?*

"The section on feelings and responses has really helped the girls," she continued. "It has helped us, too."

I nodded as I realised, she was talking about the grief and loss program.

"Yesterday my husband received the tragic news that his best mate had been killed in a motorbike accident," she continued. Her lips were quivering. "He's a tough bloke," she said. "But it was all too much for him. He just broke down."

My head shook as I closed my eyes. *How much does this family have to bear? Life or tragedy doesn't stop just because there's been a flood.* "I'm so sorry to hear that," I replied. "Is there anything we can do to help?"

Her face brightened. "I was able to comfort him with the words the girls had shared from the program," she continued. "I told him that his feelings were normal; a natural response to what's happened."

I took a deep breath. "It is a natural response," I repeated. "It still doesn't make it easy."

The children and young people were able to draw and share their stories of change and loss caused by the natural disaster. The program enabled them to understand their feelings and develop ways to adapt and recover.

Session three encouraged children to bring one of their favourite treasures to help them talk about a special memory. My heart broke as Kirsty one of the Year 7's opened the box. She had arrived early and bounded into the kitchen.

"I had a set of precious stones collected over the years," she said. "Someone gave me these to replace mine that were washed away in the flood. Aren't they beautiful?"

As the realisation the young people had lost everything, arose, I gasped. *How can they bring a favourite treasure when they have lost the basics? Why didn't I think?*

"I like this one," she said as she picked up an opaque coloured stone.

"It's beautiful," I responded.

Kirsty's strength and resilience astounded me. She often helped and comforted the younger children and set a wonderful model of behaviour amongst her peers. She had an incredibly strong mental attitude.

"It must have been hard to lose everything," I said as we continued lining up the rocks on the bench.

"My dad was part of the rescue," she said. "He got in his boat and pulled as many to safety as he could. He said it was difficult and frightening as the

Chapter 23 | The Garden

water was raging. We all headed to the school for safety. We're lucky we all got out."

"You demonstrate the same strength and courage as your dad," I replied as I looked her in the eye. "We're lucky to have young people like you in our community."

As I walked into the office Carly was standing at the photocopier, smiling as though she had just been nominated Principal of the Year.

"What do you think of this?" she asked as she handed me a folded card.

I could hear children clambering down the stairs as I stood marvelling at the collage of photos of dignitaries and donors who had visited the school throughout the year.

"This is so good," I replied. "You've captured it so well."

"Turn it over," Carly continued. "I've written a thank you letter on the back. If you fold it in three, there's room for the children to decorate the front."

"What a great way to thank the donors and for the kids to give back," I replied.

I paused.

I held my breath.

My mind ticked.

"We're going to need about three hundred cards," I continued.

"I'm sure you're up to it," she replied as her smile broadened.

The children willingly gave up their playtime for weeks to decorate each thank you card with stickers, glitter, drawings and thank you messages. The area was a hive of activity as they chatted about their favourite visitors, camps, bus trips, and special things they had received after the flood.

They never tired or complained about how many they had to do. As we were nearing the end, we encouraged the children who arrived early to school to finish them off. A sense of satisfaction washed over me as I placed the large box on Carly's desk.

"They're all done!"

***

As we headed into the last school term for the year my mind was restless. My school in Brisbane needed me to make a decision regarding the following year so they could negotiate my chaplaincy role.

Things were hectic traveling back and forth and supporting Shaz when I was home. Laura a teacher from the school and her husband Derrick let me stay in a little cottage on their property a couple of times a week which helped. *I've got a decision to make. And only I can make it.*

"There's so much more to be done," I said to Lilly as I sat looking out of the school window. "They haven't even had the first memorial. I'm going to need another year."

***

The children had not long started the school year when there was more torrential rain. Everyone was on edge as the rain pelted for hours. The phone was ringing hot.

"Can we still get through?" a parent asked anxiously. "Should we come now to collect the children?"

I ran down to the railway bridge.

"The water's only ankle deep," I said breathlessly having run back up the hill. "We need to reassure the parents, and the children."

The tension in the air was thick as the fear on the children's faces increased.

"I can't believe this is happening again," I said to Ruby, Carly's replacement as she gave me a list of families to call.

After a hectic year Carly had transitioned to another school. Ruby was teaching the upper grades; the year prior so was well-acquainted with the trauma the children had been through.

My ears were attuned to the wind blustering as it competed with the rain.

"There's still access, at this stage," I said to one of the parents on the phone. "We're keeping a close eye on the road."

"You can collect the children earlier if you're worried," I continued. "We'll just need to sign them out when you get here."

I looked at the list.

Chapter 23 | The Garden

Fifteen to go.

The following days were stressful as the rain continued to pour. *This is unbelievable. This must be terrifying for the families after last year.*

The rain eventually stopped, though the anxiety in the children took a while to subside. Normality eventually returned as they realised they were safe.

***

One afternoon I noticed Ruby standing at the garden bed at the bottom of the staff carpark.

"Dale's dad wants us to build a memorial garden in the school to remember the family," she said. "We've talked about it for a while and I think it's the right time."

I stood silently looking at the concrete blocks surrounding the mound of dirt.

"It might bring a lot of emotions to the surface," I responded. "The children are a lot more settled, but the trauma is never far from their minds. How do you think Dale will go?"

"I think we should get him involved," she replied. "It'll be hard, but I think it'll be good for him too."

"Mum's favourite flowers were yellow roses," Dale said as we sat painting the bricks around the garden edge.

It was only the second time I had heard him talk about her.

"Were they?" I replied. "Would you like to plant a few in the garden?"

He nodded.

"What was your brother's favourite colour?" I asked.

His cheeky grin had returned. "Pink of course," he responded with a glint in his eye.

"Of course," I replied. "What about your sister?"

He stood still for a moment. Shrugging his shoulders, he turned towards Bruce, who was helping us paint.

"Ask Bruce," he replied. "He'll know."

The garden slowly emerged as the groundsman poured in the soil. One by one Dale and a few of his friends planted his mum's favourite roses.

As I sat in the cool of the evening finishing off the final layer, I thanked God for the opportunity he had given me to support a community that had been through so much suffering.

The children and their families gathered around the garden the following morning. The yellow, pink, and white roses looked radiant amidst the complementing shrubs.

A lump formed in my throat as Dale and his dad placed the photos of his family in the centre of the garden. Tears were rolling down faces as we all stood silently.

"They've been so brave." I whispered to Ruby. "I don't know how they do it each day."

The answer was clear as I thought about Sharyn and our own journey. *One day at a time.*

***

As the year was coming to an end, my emotions were scattered like the cups I had collected the first day we ran the breakfast program.

"It's time for me to head back to Brisbane," I said to Ruby as I sat in her office. "There's a lot going on where Sharyn lives, and I need to get my feet back on the ground there."

Her countenance dropped as my words registered.

"I'm happy to work the first term next year to help the children settle in," I continued. "I don't want to leave without having a replacement."

She took her time to find her words. "I'm so sorry to hear that," she replied, "but I understand. It's been so great to have you here. I don't know how we would have made it through without your support."

I looked back at her with a gentle smile. "Thanks," I replied. "I feel so honoured. It's been great to be able to do something small to help. It's such a strong, resilient community."

A sense of relief washed over me when I heard one of the high school chaplains had been appointed. I could leave knowing that support for the school community would continue.

Chapter 23 | The Garden

***

My last day was full of mixed emotions. I had carried the community in my heart for two years. The children had become precious treasures as we walked alongside them helping them to heal, recover and rebuild their lives.

Families and community supporters were starting to arrive for my farewell afternoon tea. As I stood chatting on the verandah, one of the mothers moved towards me with her three children.

"I just wanted to say thank you for all that you have done for our family," she said as she handed me a bunch of flowers.

My throat constricted as I held back the tears. I felt completely overwhelmed. This little family had lost so much. I didn't know what to say. A hug for each of them would have to be enough.

Deanne one of the local church ministers must have seen my face go pale as I tried to find somewhere to pull myself together.

"Are you okay?" she asked.

I burst into tears. I was gulping for air. I couldn't speak.

She wrapped her arms around me.

"You've done an amazing job," she whispered.

Stepping back as she handed me a tissue I asked, "How am I going to say goodbye to these people?" I wiped my eyes as I took a deep breath. "I feel so honoured that they have let me into their lives. They've all been through so much."

Deanne looked at her watch. "It's nearly three thirty. We need to get you inside."

My hand was shaking as I stood at the front acknowledging foodbank, the church ministers and other local organisations who had supported my role in the school.

I thanked Laura and Derrick who let me stay in the little cottage on their property, easing my need to travel back and forth from Brisbane each day. They became a second family as we shared meals together on the nights I was there.

I finished thanking the staff, the children, and their families for allowing me to serve them through such a challenging season.

As I hopped in my car with packed up resources and gifts, I realised there was someone at home who needed me more than ever right now. Shaz.

CHAPTER 24
The Yellow Envelope

Paintings on the walls were replaced with new ones. Ideas were put on the table, even though they had been trialled years before and found to be unsuccessful for our specific demographic group. The height adjustable chairs with backs were replaced with stools without backs, again. It was the third management change in a year.

The warm smell of roast chicken and vegetables filtered down the hallway. Staff were standing behind the tables ready to serve. Christmas Carols played in the background seeking to lighten the mood.

"Who's that in the red shirt?" Mum asked as we sat with Shaz in the midst of the festivities.

I rolled my eyes.

"Don't bother learning her name," I replied. "She'll be gone before you remember it."

Mum chuckled.

Daisy Lodge was like a revolving door. The therapists rotated as regularly as the managers. Each one came wanting to put their own stamp on the place. The constant changes slowly eroded the staff morale and philosophy of care. The mission statement had been removed. We were on a roundabout with no hope of getting off, but at least Sharyn had somewhere to live and her nursing staff were consistent and very kind.

Mum introduced herself as she lined up to be served.

"I'm Sharyn's Mum," she said as she held out her plate. "I haven't met you before."

"Hi, I'm Rebecca, the physiotherapist," she replied as she picked up a couple of pieces of roast beef with the tongs, "but I'm leaving tomorrow."

I coughed.

As we moved towards the salads, I turned to mum and gave her an uneven smile.

I told you.

***

After eight years at Daisy Lodge the Government of the day had built the young people living with Acquired Brain Injury a new facility. The name Daisy Lodge was retained.

Sharyn and other residents finally had their own rooms. They were small but theirs to make their own. Resident's equipment lined the hallways, tucked under a cupboard that housed their day to day necessities.

They were at the new facility for five years when uncertainty reared its head, again. Our family members were gathered in the common area for the special meeting.

"The State Government is building two new wings at one of the hospitals," the director of nursing said. "We're advocating for one wing to be allocated to Acquired Brain Injury to accommodate your family members."

I could see the look of exasperation creeping onto our parents' faces. I felt the same way. *This is so unfair. Why are they doing this? Haven't they just built us this new facility?*

Families collaborated after the meeting to share their distress and look for ways the decision could be overturned. The change was not guaranteed but appeared to be imminent.

"We need to keep the residents together," one of the parents said. "They have specific needs, requiring specialised staff to care for them. We need to be strong and agree that we'll only go if they can remain together."

Chapter 24 | The Yellow Envelope

Under duress, our families agreed.

The thought of having to uproot again unsettled me. We had done it thirteen years ago in order to be closer to Shaz and now we were facing another move.

After a few more meetings, the weeks rolled into months with nothing further eventuating. We subsequently learned the wing had been allocated to aged care. We went back to our daily lives, but the shadow always loomed.

***

We had another six years reprieve before the long-term security was again shaken.

"They're going to put our family members back into aged care," Annabelle said as I answered the phone.

"What do you mean?" I responded. "How do you know that?"

Her voice quivered. "I rang the nurse unit manager to ask about Veronica's washing," she replied. "She just blurted it on the phone."

My heart sank. *Not again.*

"Leave it with me." I responded. "Mum and I haven't met her yet. I'll request a meeting."

I stood still as my eyes caught sight of the director of nursing. "Why's she here?" I whispered to Mum as we sat in the foyer, "we've only requested a meeting to meet and greet the new nurse unit manager. They're well prepared. They must be on to us."

The director of nursing followed us in as Mum and I wriggled into the manager's small room. The air was stuffy. I moved my fingers to loosen my top from around my neck.

"Can I please ask where the directive to transition our residents back to age care is coming from?" I asked the unit manager in a firm tone. "Is it the district or the health department?"

The director of nursing gave her a fleeting look.

"It's a State Government initiative," she replied.

"Is it possible to give me a name and contact number of the person in charge?" I continued, "or do I need to find it myself?"

Silence filled the room. I could hear the receptionist moving folders outside. I barely blinked as I sat waiting with my arms folded.

"I can provide it," the nurse unit manager responded. "I'll email it this afternoon."

You could hear the large portion of air that had built up in my lungs exhaling through my nose.

"It's not going to be easy," I said to Mum as we left the meeting. "We need advice. I'm going to call Melinda the CEO of Youth Care."

A number of our families had met her and a colleague a few months earlier. They represented an organisation who fundraised and established group homes for young people misplacd in nursing homes. I fervently searched around for her business card.

Melinda remembered us instantly. "How's everything?" she asked.

"Our parents are distressed," I replied. "We've been told there's a state government directive to transition our residents back into aged care. Mum and other families fought so hard to get them out twenty years ago. They won't live through seeing them returned."

"Let me have a chat with Greg, a representative from disability services," she said. "I have a direct line to him. Can you ring him this afternoon? I'll ask him to take your call."

My hand was on my chest.

"Yes, I can?" I replied. "That's amazing. Thank you so much."

I was surprised when he called me an hour later.

"Hi Nyree, It's Greg, a representative from disabilities services. Melinda has asked me to give you a call. She's given me the rundown on your concerns about residents being returned to aged care."

"My boss is meeting with a representative from the department of health tonight," he continued. "I'll advise you of the outcome once they've spoken."

"Thank you," I replied as I slowly put down the receiver. I stood staring at the phone. *Did that really happen?*

The following day Greg called me back. "The process of discharge planning has been halted on instruction from the department," he stated.

"Management have not followed correct procedures. We've asked them to reinstate the family/carer meetings bi-monthly to ensure adequate communication and consultation continues with the residents and their families."

It was the first and last time I spoke to him, as we had a change of government the following year.

I had met both candidates prior to the election. "I've only had to knock on the door twice in twenty years," I said to both of them. "Hopefully we won't have to knock on yours, but if we do you know who I am and who I represent."

It was a landslide election with the opposition government regaining power. Unfortunately, it was only eighteen months before I was knocking again, to request an appointment.

My stress levels had skyrocketed due to the decline in service at Daisy Lodge. My head was throbbing, my back was aching. I knelt beside my bed. All I could do was cry. A groan flooding from my stomach squeezed through the tightness in my throat.

"You're a righteous, just, and fair God." I cried. "This isn't right, it isn't just, it isn't fair." I paused. "I need your wisdom. I need your protection. I need your grace."

***

The following morning, I sat in church feeling fatigued.

Washed out.

Hopeless.

Shaun, the senior pastor, was preaching on Acts Chapter 18. As he started to share cultural information on Corinth, the words from the Bible leapt off the page and hit me in the stomach.

> One night the Lord spoke to Paul in a vision: "Do not be afraid: keep on speaking, do not be silent. For I am with you, and no one is going to attack and harm you because I have many people in this city."

Tingles went through my body, my heart began to pound. *I can't stay silent. Sharyn and the others don't have a voice. I need to keep going.* I closed my eyes. "Please give me the courage, Jesus," I prayed.

***

The next day I stood nervously in the state member's office. "What did you do before you worked here?" I asked the electoral officer.

"I was a church minister," he replied. "For seventeen years."

I looked back at him wide-eyed, as I gave him a nod. *He's a Christian.*

He joined the meeting with a notebook and pen in hand.

I felt flushed. The door was shut restricting the airflow. My heart was beating faster than usual.

The yellow envelope sat on the table beside me.

"I'm dealing with multiple levels of government," I said to the state member. "I'm not getting anywhere. I have an external advisor. I need an internal one."

The electoral officer reached over to pour me a glass of water.

"It's so bad" I continued, "our families have gone to the quality and complaints department."

The atmosphere in the room changed. They both sat upright giving each other a fleeting glance. The silence was palpable. The state member looked back at me. His lips tightened.

I sat silently wondering if I should continue.

He glanced at the yellow envelope, before breaking the silence. "What's going on up there?" he asked.

"They've cut Daisy Lodge in half," I replied, "without any notification. Access to the outside now sits on the other side of the door. The residents no longer have natural light in their common area."

I closed my eyes for a moment and took a breath. "Some of the residents aren't getting out of bed and if they do it's only for a few hours," I continued. "Some are only getting a shower every second day."

He leant forward but remained silent allowing me to continue.

"Their food isn't adequate or nutritious."

My throat started to choke as tears came to the surface. "Community access, activities, and therapy have been removed. The services are only being offered to patients in the new wing."

I bent over to reach for a tissue in my bag and gently blew my nose.

"We're fighting for basic human rights."

"Have you raised it with the unit manager?" he asked.

Fury engulfed me as I stared back at him.

"We've raised it with five levels of government," I replied. "The quality and complaints department was our last resort."

I moved the yellow envelope towards him. "Five families have complained," I said. "I have copies for your reference."

He pulled the envelope towards him. "I'm going to need some time to look into this," he replied. "My office will respond in the next few days."

I felt like I had been through the wringer as I walked out. My energy was flat, my mind quiet. *It's going to take more than lollies to get me through this.*

CHAPTER 25
Seeing Red

When the residents first moved to Daisy Lodge a number of family members formed an incorporated association. Mum, Maureen, her husband Harry and a few others family members advocated and raised money to donate items that would benefit the residents not otherwise provided within the system.

The group had met David, the CEO of Community Care, who provide housing for people living with disabilities, six months prior to Daisy Lodge being cut in half. He was a warm man with a measured countenance. He graciously listened as I shared our story.

"We recently visited one of your group homes," I said. "We observed a level of care our family members used to have."

His eyes sparkled as he took in the compliment.

"Sadly, the care of our residents has declined over the years," I continued. "Their parents are ageing. They're distressed."

"Every five years we face the uncertainty of where our loved ones are going to live. A couple of years ago they tried to transition them back to aged care and now the state government have stated it may not be feasible to continue services at Daisy Lodge, due to the closure of an adjoining nursing home."

I glanced at the chart of values hanging on the wall. Looking back at him I said, "We can't keep living with this uncertainty. Is there any way your organisation can help us?"

Compassion oozed out of his eyes as he swivelled in his chair and looked towards Mum and Maureen. He gave them a gentle smile.

"I want to commend you ladies for the years you've endured and cared for your loved ones," he replied. "I can't imagine what you've been through."

"I'll need to have a chat with our board," he continued. "I can't give you any guarantees, but we'll see if we can support you in some way."

***

I nearly jumped through the roof when I received an email from him a few days later.

> We'd like to meet with your small group again to scope out a potential action plan for finding a new home and appropriate long-term staffing and care environment for your residents. Until we spend more time with your group, we won't know whether we can address all of the complexities that will achieve that vision. But we'd like to work with you on that journey.

As we returned to his office, we were introduced to Geraldine – a staff member who was assigned to work with us.

Geraldine's words took me by surprise. On one hand I was fighting for our residents with everything within me and on the other I was freely receiving her kindness, understanding, wisdom, and care with the backing of her organisation, who were trying to support us. It all seemed too good to be true.

Our group spent the next few months developing options for local supported accommodation, considering the individual needs of each resident that would provide a quality lifestyle.

The day the government cut Daisy Lodge in half; I rang Geraldine in desperation.

"I need to go to the media," I said. "Can you help me?"

Chapter 25 | Seeing Red

Geraldine had worked in the disability industry for over twenty years before taking on her new role. She knew every procedure and policy and was willing to pass on the guidance.

"You only get one chance with the media," she replied. "I know the short-term situation is bad and needs to be fixed, but you also need a long-term solution. If you go to the media now you won't get a second opportunity."

As I started to calm down I sat back in my chair. "Okay," I replied.

"You need to speak with your state member about long term options," she continued. "I'll help you draft a proposal. You need to get him raising the need for land, capital and operational funding with the Department of Health and Disability Services."

Communication and meetings with the state member became a regular occurrence over the following months. He was young, but knew his position and authority and acted on everything we requested.

We used all available means to pursue a long-term solution, whilst fighting for basic day to day care for the residents at Daisy Lodge.

"They'll do everything to wear you out," Geraldine said. "They'll be hoping you'll eventually run out of steam."

"That won't be happening," I replied. "I've resigned from my job and am determined I won't be going back to work until I get the residents out of there. I might get weary, but I won't give up. They are one of the most vulnerable groups in society and deserve to be looked after."

Little did I know how much energy would be required and how long it would take.

***

The angry protesters were shouting as I turned the corner. Fear rose in my heart as I watched them push their placards in the air. I stopped the car. *Will I get past? Will I be safe?*

I took the risk. I walked briskly towards the building. The noise dropped as the automatic doors shut behind me.

As I entered the room, a representative from an Australian lobby group caught my eye. I greeted her before taking a seat.

Questions filled with passion and fury were being shot at the state treasurer who was facilitating the forum on the state's budget.

I watched his every move, his facial muscles and his body language. *He's holding himself well. You've got to have tough skin to be a politician. I wouldn't like to be in his shoes.*

Looking at the clock I raised my hand thirty minutes before the forum was due to end. Someone else was picked. I tried to lift my hand a little higher. I didn't take my eyes off the adjudicator.

My pleading look must have caught his attention. "The last question will be from the woman in red," he said.

"Thank you," I whispered as I relaxed and returned a smile.

I could hear my heart beating in my chest as he signalled for me to speak. My mind flashed back to the day mum pleaded with the Health Minister in the mall twenty-four years earlier when Sharyn had nowhere to live.

I took a deep breath.

"I represent a group of people living with Acquired Brain Injury," I said. "They're a tiny part of your budget. We have a solution, but no department is willing to listen."

"You need to raise it with the health department in your region," he replied.

"I've done that," I stated in a firm tone.

"Have you spoken to your state member?" he asked.

I nodded my head.

"I've done that, too."

He finally conceded. "You can come down the front and speak to Aaron after the meeting," he replied. "He'll take your details."

I shifted my weight from leg to leg as I quietly waited in the line.

"Can you put your request in writing?" Aaron asked as I spoke to him about the government land solutions. He handed me his card.

***

Chapter 25 | Seeing Red

The representative from the Australian lobby group rang me a couple of days later. "I'm hosting a forum with representatives from Communities, Child Safety and Disability Services next week," she said. "If you register, I'll give you the opportunity to ask one question. You'll need to email me the question for the panel by Friday."

Geraldine had helped me with my preparation but my nerves escalated the minute I walked into the room. Multiple microphones lined the long tables at the front, with government representatives from varying departments sitting behind them. I read and reread my question.

"It's been great to hear how your department has allocated funding to enable people with low to moderate needs to be transitioned to community-based living," I said projecting my voice as far as I could.

"I represent people with high and complex needs. What is the government doing now to ensure people with high and complex needs have access to appropriate housing and support options?"

The representative paused as she looked back at me. "Do you represent residents from Daisy Lodge?"

I was stopped in my tracks. *How did she know? Our message must be getting through somewhere.*

Putting my shoulders back I replied. "Yes, I do."

She signalled with her hand as she asked me to come down and speak to her after the meeting.

"Our state member has been in contact with your department regarding the elderly parent scheme," I said.

She became a little agitated as people started to gather to speak to her. "I can't discuss it tonight as I have others waiting to see me," she replied.

I was desperate. I had an audience with her and as far as I was concerned Sharyn and the other residents were the most important issue. *Everyone else will have to wait.*

Tears were forming in my eyes as I pleaded with her.

"My office will be in contact with your state member," she replied as she started to walk away.

I felt like I was going around in circles but I didn't give up.

***

A further meeting was scheduled with Charles an official representative from the health department. Our little advocacy group met to prepare.

"We need to discuss the long-term issue first," Harry, Maureen's husband, said. "We can only have one speaker." He looked at me. "I think Nyree should speak as she has all of the information on the proposal."

Anxiety filled my mind. "I need you to sit next to me." I replied. "I need you to prod me if I get off track."

I looked towards Mum. I knew she could fire up in these meetings as she had advocated for the original facility.

"We might have to tape Mum's mouth," I said with a chuckle, "or write the word in front of her to remind her not to speak."

My heart warmed when Charles entered the room. He looked like a huggable grandfather anyone would want to call their own.

He walked around the room and shook everyone's hand. His gentle smile beamed from his cheeks.

I glanced down at the first item on our agenda. "We're sourcing alternative options for our loved ones," I said. "The State Government has a number of schemes that can support land and capital. We need to secure recurrent funding to be able to progress."

"Funding residential care isn't a state government function," he replied.

The room fell silent. I could see mum's lips moving. I lifted my fingers to remind her about the tape.

"It is a state government responsibility," I replied. "Our family members are living in a state government facility and have done so for twenty-three years." I could feel my temperature rising. "They're not even getting a daily shower at the moment."

His jolly countenance turned serious. He glanced towards Donna his liaison officer.

She gave him a nod to validate the statement.

His response revealed he was unaware of the matters being escalated through the various levels of management under his governance. He reverted back to the long-term issue.

"We've had a directive from the health department to collaborate with other government departments to move forward with the Action Plan," he said.

My mind clambered. *What's the Action Plan? This one hasn't come up before.*

"We'll continue to accommodate the residents where they are," he continued, "and address the concerns you have raised regarding the quality of daily care."

I was less than satisfied but at least this was a starting point.

"Can I have a copy of the Action Plan," I asked Donna as we left the meeting.

"It's not a public document," she replied. "Its purpose is to work collaboratively to transition long-stay young people with a disability out of the public health facilities in Queensland."

We had been on the roundabout for twelve months and there was no hope of getting off. The circle was tiresome, but I had to keep going.

***

Three days after Christmas the state member forwarded a response from the health minister regarding our request for supported housing solutions in our community.

> Referring to our meeting with Charles the health representative a few months earlier he stated: "Miss Mannion noted that ongoing residence in a state government facility is not a viable option given residential care is the responsibility of the federal government."

I saw red. *I can't believe they're putting my name to it. Not only are they mistreating our people they're misrepresenting me.*

I wasn't about to take this lying down. A copy of the National Health Reform Agreement was in front of me. To protect myself, I wrote to the federal member for clarification. It took three months for a reply but the letter couldn't have come at a better time.

CHAPTER 26
Home for Life

The health department had commissioned an external review for Daisy Lodge to assess the day to day concerns raised by family members, objectively and with clarity. Over the course of the week, interviews were held with staff, residents, family members, specific heads of departments and clinical directors. Internal and external documents were reviewed for evidence.

A couple of months later families were called to a meeting to discuss the recommendations. On arrival I was introduced to a media representative. *Why have they got the media here?*

I noticed a number of family members scattered around the room. *How much longer do we have to do this? I'm so tired.* I sat down towards the back and started to doodle on the blank page in front of me.

The health representative commenced the meeting with a formal apology. I lifted my head as his words arrested my attention. *Did he just apologise? Are they admitting to it? That's incredible. I never thought government departments did that. No wonder the media representative is here.*

Three well-dressed men were sitting to the side of him. Their faces were serious. He spoke about the recommendations and what the health department had planned.

He moved towards our resident's long-term future. "Residential care is not a state government responsibility," he stated.

My hand and mouth moved before my brain had time to catch up.

"Sorry," I called out in a loud tone as I stood up. "Can I please address that comment? I wrote to our Federal Member for clarity on this issue."

I opened the letter that had arrived that morning and started to read.

> The new National Health Reform Agreement finalized by the State, Territory and Commonwealth Governments in August 2011 states: the Commonwealth will be responsible for aged care services (for people aged 65 years and over, 50 years and over for Aboriginal and Torres Strait Islander peoples); and the State for disability and community services (for those aged under 65 years; and under 50 years for Aboriginal and Torres Strait Islander peoples).

"Can I please have a look?" one of the men at the front asked as he stretched out his hand.

"Yes," I responded. "I've got copies for you."

The room went silent. I sat down marvelling that the letter had arrived that day. *Thank you, God, you've done it again.*

We were handed a copy of the report at the conclusion of the meeting. I slipped it into my bag and couldn't wait to get home to read it.

As I looked at the words, grief gripped my heart.

> The change directly resulted in the longer-term residents having some of their fundamental rights deprived; primarily personal care and hygiene, access to adequate food and outside fresh air, including environmental changes to the unit itself.

My head was shaking. *This is a systemic breakdown.* I was interrupted as Mum arrived home.

That evening I sat silently wading through the recommendations. *We've got a long way to go but things will change.*

***

Chapter 26 | Home for Life

A week later we returned to meet with David and Geraldine from Community Care to report back on our progress and discuss further options for long-term housing.

I avoided eye contact as I greeted David. I was so fragile even a compassionate look would reduce me to tears. I placed my tongue between my teeth and my lips to maintain some control.

"These ladies have had a big year," Geraldine said. "They engaged the state member to advocate government on their behalf. Nyree has raised their plight at public forums, she instigated a hand written and online petition and used media. The families have also had an external review on the day to day services at Daisy Lodge."

My head was shaking.

"I couldn't have done it without Geraldine," I said as I half lifted my head. "She's been an incredible strength and source of wisdom."

There was no way to hold back the tears any longer.

"We're so thankful for her encouragement and support." I took a moment to regain my composure. "I would have self-destructed," I continued with a chuckle. "I was ready to go to the media on day one and every other day."

Geraldine raised her eyebrows as she nodded.

David glanced at his large whiteboard on the wall.

"I need to have another conversation with the board about providing a possible housing solution" he stated. "I can't commit to anything until I've spoken to them. If we take your families on to build them a home, we'll take them on for life."

My heart was heavy as I left the meeting. My thoughts were consumed with doubt. *They won't take our residents on. They're too complex and it's probably too expensive.*

***

A week later I stood staring at the cereal in the supermarket. I didn't know whether to scream, shout, jump or cry. Tears were welling in my eyes. I didn't know how to respond.

"Are you there?" David asked.

"I don't know what to say," I responded. "I can't believe it."

"We'll organise another meeting soon to discuss the next steps," he continued. "I'll leave it to you to tell the others. Enjoy your day."

I was too excited to finish the shopping. I purchased the few things I had in the trolley and headed to the car.

"Community Care are going to take us on!" I screamed with excitement into the phone.

"What are you talking about?" Mum asked.

"David, he's just called me. I can't believe it. They're going to build Shaz and the others a new home."

"I need to call Geraldine," I continued. "I'll see you when I get home. Can you let the others know?"

***

A couple of months later we were heading into another meeting. We had attended so many, but I knew this one would be different.

"I feel so relieved," I said to Harry as we waited for David to arrive. "We're not on our own anymore."

"I've opted for a shorter proposal rather than providing too much detail," David said as he handed us a copy. "I want to leave them with a real option to think about and hope they might come back asking us for a more detailed proposal."

We filed into the meeting room and sat down at the long table. David spoke on our behalf.

I clicked my heels under the table as the disability services representative indicated we would have to submit a formal proposal.

He placed a copy on the table.

The following week we received an email from the Department of Disability Services. They had been endorsed to proceed with more detailed planning on the proposal from Community Care to build a home to accommodate up to ten residents from Daisy Lodge. It was to include capital and operational funding.

Chapter 26 | Home for Life

Our fight was almost over. After being tossed to and fro for more than twenty years, the promise of a home for life for our loved ones was shaping up to becoming a reality.

Services were gradually being improved at Daisy Lodge. The weight of an uncertain future was gone. Hope was being restored.

***

The ensuing eighteen months were brighter. Harry and I represented families on the project control group for the development of the new home. Community Care carried a respect and a genuine care for our loved ones and their family members.

With increased energy, I was like a horse ready to bolt. I wanted to shout about the new home from the rooftops.

I was hemmed in by the need to wait for the development application to be approved, so I turned my energy towards another project.

Reading the local paper, I saw an article, "Help give Jeremy a lift." I recognised the family as I had chatted with them on a number of occasions after church.

I did a few sums. *Having a modified van had changed our lives. It would change theirs, too. Fundraising for Jeremy would open doors for when we are ready to raise support for the new home.*

"Do you know what type of vehicle you are looking for and an approximate cost?" I said to Ben and Andrea one afternoon after the church service. "I've got some time on my hands, I'd be happy to help you."

Ben and Andrea had already done their homework. Their son Jeremy had a brain tumour removed when he was eighteen months of age. He suffered post-operative complications causing brain injury.

Jeremy was fifteen and approximately sixty-five kilos. He was able to weight bear, but was unable to walk. The family were becoming desperate as they physically lifted him in and out of their car daily.

"I didn't realise there were so many needs in our community," I said to Sophie one of the ladies helping me with the fundraising strategy. "Look at this little guy," I said as I handed her the newspaper article. "His needs are more pressing than Jeremy's."

"When I was serving the community ravaged by the floods," I continued, "I discovered a great secret. The local community were fundraising for a young girl who had a rare type of Leukaemia and needed to go to Germany for specialised treatment."

"Everywhere I turned I saw promotions, raising money for Nancy. On the sign entering town, on the school sign, at the RSL. Someone had to be driving the project. We can do the same for Jeremy."

Sophie and I engaged a couple of like-minded friends and raised support wherever we could. Over the following six months we promoted Jeremy's needs through the local paper, businesses, the Chamber of Commerce, markets, community groups and hosted a number of community events.

The car handover was a special day. As I stood looking at the bright blue bow wrapped around the vehicle, I smiled. *This is going to change this family's life and open up so many new opportunities, just as our vehicle did so many years ago.*

Jeremy's face was beaming as I stood with his family thanking everyone who had made it possible.

I felt so fulfilled as they loaded him into the back and drove off with arms waving in every direction. *It took longer than I expected, but it was worth it.*

***

A few months later we were given the green light to share our story that Community Care were building residents from Daisy Lodge a new home. The good news was finally out. "A Home for Life." We wrote to every single person who had signed our community petition and timed it with the newspaper article.

The story was bittersweet for some. One of our local churches had closed its doors the same year we were in the height of our advocacy. The minister of the overarching church and David the CEO of Community Care had run into each other at a regional meeting.

A chance conversation caused them to realise the land would meet the need for our development. The elderly congregation were pleased the land they had met on for so many years, hosting church, marriages, baptism and funerals would continue to support the most vulnerable in their community.

Chapter 26 | Home for Life

***

"I can't believe this is happening," I whispered to Mum as we sat on the white chairs under the marquee. "I didn't think this day would ever come."

Our eldest family member who had visited her son daily for over thirty years and I were invited to turn the sod with the CEO, the Minister for Disability and the State Member.

"Watch my shoes," I joked as the Minister for Disability turned the shovel. "They're new."

My heart was full of gratitude as I looked at our families. *They've been through so much heartache for so many years. A new facility won't fix the disability but it will bring peace and hope that we never have to face an uncertain future again.*

"Our loved ones have finally got a place to call home" I said to mum.

"You did it" mum beamed.

"We did!"

"END"

Epilogue

Nyree, her mum and local community members went on to develop an organisation called Make it Home Safely Inc to raise the awareness of the long-term impact of traumatic head injury and to empower young people to create, communicate and implement safe driving practices. A team of volunteers ran community events and a high school education program to improve attitude and driving behaviour.

Receiving the donation of two vehicles, Nyree and her volunteers moved into supporting disadvantaged young people without access to a supervisor or registered vehicle to complete the logbook hours to obtain their provisional licence.

www.makeithome.com.au

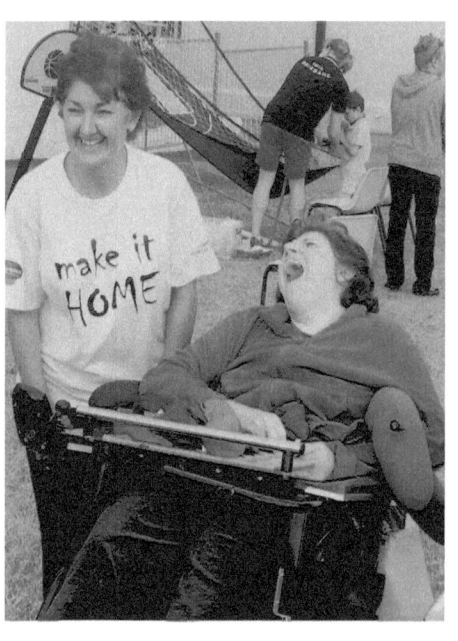

About the Author

Nyree Mannion is a determined, adventurous lady who loves opportunity and will give anything a go. As a young person she worked in receptionist roles before becoming a sales representative in the travel industry.

Nyree experienced a family tragedy at a young age. Upon finding faith she stepped out of full-time work at the age of twenty-six to attend Bible College and went on to complete a Bachelor of Ministry.

Her life priorities became serving God, her community and supporting her family. Nyree worked with children teaching religious instruction, establishing Kids' Club, leading camps and serving as a school chaplain.

She participated in short- and long-term missions and worked with a small group of people to develop a new community church.

Her passion and strong sense of justice compelled Nyree to advocate for her sister and other vulnerable young people living with Acquired Brain Injury. She also fostered children.

Nyree's life demonstrates that with courage, compassion, determination and love you can do anything no matter what the cost.

www.ingramcontent.com/pod-product-compliance
Lightning Source LLC
Chambersburg PA
CBHW021948290426
44108CB00012B/992